THE BEATITUDES FOR TODAY

THE BEATITUDES FOR TODAY

James C. Howell

WESTMINSTER
JOHN KNOX PRESS
LOUISVILLE • KENTUCKY

© 2006 James C. Howell

Scripture quotations from the Revised Standard Version of the Bible are copyright © 1946, 1952, 1971, and 1973 by the Division of Christian Education of the National Council of the Churches of Christ in the U.S.A. and are used by permission.

Book design by Sharon Adams
Cover design by Eric Walljasper, Minneapolis, MN

First edition
Published by Westminster John Knox Press
Louisville, Kentucky

This book is printed on acid-free paper that meets the American National Standards Institute Z39.48 standard. ⊚

PRINTED IN THE UNITED STATES OF AMERICA

08 09 10 11 12 13 14 15—10 9 8 7 6 5 4

Library of Congress Cataloging-in-Publication Data is on file at the Library of Congress, Washington, D.C.

ISBN-13: 978-0-664-22932-0
ISBN-10: 0-664-22932-8

To Randy and Tom

Contents

Series Introduction

*T*he For Today series is intended to provide reliable and accessible resources for the study of important biblical texts, theological documents, and Christian practices. The series is written by experts who are committed to making the results of their studies available to those with no particular biblical or theological training. The goal is to provide an engaging means to study texts and practices that are familiar to laity in churches. The authors are all committed to the importance of their topics and to communicating the significance of their understandings to a wide audience. The emphasis is not only on what these subjects have meant in the past but also on their value in the present—"For Today."

Our hope is that the books in this series will find eager readers in churches, particularly in the context of education classes. The authors are educators and pastors who wish to engage church laity in the issues raised by their topics. They seek to provide guidance for learning, for nurture, and for growth in Christian experience.

To enhance the educational usefulness of these volumes, Questions for Discussion are included at the end of each chapter.

We hope the books in this series will be important resources to enhance Christian faith and life.

The Publisher

1

What Jesus Didn't Say

"*T*hese [people] who have turned the world upside down have come here also!" So shouted a highly offended, ferocious mob back during the heyday of the Roman Empire. What had provoked them? Assassins of another Caesar usurping power? Terrorist raiders from Parthia firing arrows? Witches in league with the powers of the underworld? Incredibly, the threat had come from a couple of ex-convicts, who had just gotten out of jail in a Macedonian town called Philippi, where they had been charged with "disturbing our city." Surviving a severe beating, Paul and Silas managed to get extricated from prison and to walk a hundred miles to Thessalonica, which would hardly be the last city in which they touched off a small riot.

The Greco-Roman world had seen a few radical teachers come and go, and those in power knew how to deal with them. The genius Socrates once badgered Callicles into a corner until in exasperation he admitted, "O Socrates, if what you say is true, then the life of us mortals must be turned upside down, and we are everywhere doing the opposite of what we should."[1] Socrates wound up being forced to drink hemlock for suggesting the Athenians had gotten not just a few things, but everything, backwards.

The Teacher that Paul and Silas professed to follow had been even more gruesomely executed by the iron fist of Rome. Jesus had rudely crumpled up the mental map of the known world, and nobody in Galilee or Jerusalem seemed to appreciate having their traditional view of the world refolded and then redrawn, as if by some spiritual origami. And so, those who followed

Jesus (and they did not linger for long in their old lives once they met Jesus) fanned out all over the Mediterranean, and in every place they were greeted with puzzled grimaces and clenched fists. "These [people] who have turned the world upside down have come here also" (Acts 17:6).

How odd all of this may seem to us! Christianity is something many nice people do, and it seems pleasant enough, so innocuous to onlookers that the potential for a riot is nonexistent. Churches do not turn the world upside down; by our architecture, dress, and behavior we fit snugly into our surroundings. Political candidates wear their faith on their sleeves. Teenagers wear bracelets that hint at some vague morality: What would Jesus do? Books on the second coming of Jesus and a movie about his death haul in millions of dollars. How did the Jesus who got his followers into constant trouble in the ancient world come to fit in so comfortably, and even successfully, in our world today? Did Jesus adapt himself to the changing times? Are we more holy and devout, more in sync with God, than those bloody Romans? Or have we missed something? Or everything?

How could it possibly matter today if we followed Jesus? What if we took Jesus half as seriously as did Paul and Silas? Is it even imaginable that offense would be taken by our sadly broken and steamily decadent world? Could cities be thrown into turmoil? What does Jesus want for me? And *from* me? If we look into the Beatitudes of Jesus, what will we find? And might a few things, or even everything, look different because of what he said? And might they actually *be* different, better, more true, more beautiful, more faithful? Will onlookers ever again say of us, "These [people] who have turned the world upside down have come here also"?

Conventional Wisdom

To see and hear Jesus with clarity, we need to tune out the background racket that can drown out what Jesus taught and blind us to what he did. To do so, it may be helpful to resort to a time-honored technique of reading the Bible. For the rabbis of Jesus' day, and for the earliest generations of Christian theologians, every sentence, every word, every letter in Scripture was there for a reason; nothing was superfluous. Every phrase, every consonant, was pregnant with meaning. In the same way, every silence, everything that was *not* said, was not said for a reason; every silence was pregnant with significance. So preachers and teachers did not merely ask, "What does Scripture say?" but pressed on to clarify, "What does Scripture *not* say? And can we deduce why?"

As we hear the Beatitudes amid the clutter of noise that is our culture, we may begin by asking, "What *didn't* Jesus say?" Now, an attorney might disapprove, as this "argument from silence" can lead us into guesswork and faulty inferences. And yet, since we know what Jesus said in the Beatitudes and elsewhere, we must acknowledge that so much of what we hear in our culture clangs noisily against Jesus' words. What passes as wisdom in our world is on the very map Jesus crumples up and throws away. Swamped as we are in a backwash of words, ideas, sound bites, half-truths, and slogans, we need to bracket out the din so we might hear the upside-downness of Jesus.

In our uncertain world, where "innocence is drowned; the best lack all conviction, while the worst are full of passionate intensity,"[2] people still are surprisingly ready to whisper advice in your ear. "If Mama ain't happy, ain't nobody happy." "Buy low, sell high." "God helps those who help themselves." "Don't worry, be happy." "Blood is thicker than water." "What sex is my child? It doesn't matter, just as long as it's healthy." "Stop and smell the roses." Each tidbit is a little "beatitude" if you will, a little pearl of wisdom, a statement about how things are, counsel which, if followed, will nudge you along the road to happiness, or at least alert you to the potholes.

How revolutionary was Jesus? And how countercultural? How profoundly wise are the Beatitudes? And how uncompromisingly do they cut against the grain of what our society parades as wisdom? Jesus didn't say:

> *Blessed are those who climb the corporate ladder; they will be blessed with a comfortable retirement.*
> > or
> *Blessed are those who invest shrewdly; they will own a second home on the coast.*
> > or
> *Blessed are those born into fine families; they will enjoy countless advantages.*

or

Blessed are those who shop, for they will own neat things.

Jesus never said,

Blessed are the rich.

Although many of us fall for the notion that Jesus really does see the rich as blessed (or even that Jesus was the one who blessed them with riches), we may recall that Jesus *did* say, "Blessed are the poor" (Luke 6:24), and was so impolite as to add, "Woe to you that are rich." Yet we fawn after the rich, and buy into our own little financial beatitudes (which Jesus did *not* say), such as:

A fool and his money are soon parted.

Allen Verhey notes that we are more likely to spot a rich person and say, "'Look, he's no fool; he's rich.' For, after all, a fool and his money *are* soon parted—and, therefore, anyone with money is no fool."[3] Jesus gets this all backwards, doesn't he?

Self-evident Blessings

All this conventional wisdom about being rich or good-looking is potent in our culture. But even if we recognize the superficiality of riches, there is more. Jesus never said,

Blessed are those with a superb education.

Not that education is an evil to be avoided! But the unlettered, those without access to the corridors of knowledge, seem to enjoy some privileged access to Jesus' kingdom, as we will be reminded later on.
Jesus never said,

Blessed are the free.

There is no good, no "blessing," that seems more good, more precious, than freedom. But what is freedom? The ability to do what I want to do? The capacity to worship God the way I want? Don't we fritter our freedom away in self-indulgence? And in making choices that the Bible would tag as sinful? Doesn't freedom of worship become freedom *not* to worship? Is worship about the way *I* want to worship? Or is it about God? Is life about doing what I want to do? Or is it tossing my wants in the trash bin and saying with the One who spoke the Beatitudes, "Not my will, but your will be done"? The Beatitudes are utterly uninterested in our vaunted "independence." Jesus himself was absorbed in *de*pendence upon God, and invited others into the same dependence, which alone is true freedom.

Jesus never said,

> *Blessed is America*
> or
> *Blessed are the Americans.*

Many (but hardly all) of the founders of our country were driven by a faith-filled, pious vision that America was birthed by divine providence, and many patriotic religious folks still maintain that we have a responsibility (due to our God-given power, size, and resources) to be the "chosen people," to lead the world. But the fact that Jesus lived on the other side of the world, and envisioned a kingdom that transcended every political boundary, should keep us humble. If we modestly pray, "God bless America," we cannot stop until we have added, "God bless Pakistan, France, China, the Sudan, Russia, Latvia . . ."

The American Declaration of Independence submits we have an "unalienable right" to the "pursuit of happiness." How fascinating, then, that Jesus never said,

> *Blessed are the happy.*

They seem blessed! Robert Schuller even wrote a book on the Beatitudes with the catchy, alluring title *The Be Happy Attitudes.* Nothing wrong with happiness! And many Bible versions, with lexicographical backing and sound reasoning, have translated the Greek word *makarios* at the beginning of each of Jesus' Beatitudes not as "blessed," but as "happy." The danger, I suspect, is that the word "happy" has gotten so watered down, so trivialized, so shredded into confetti, that the "happiness" we pursue has virtually nothing to do with what Jesus had in mind when he said "blessed." Ask any parent, or ask any spouse: "What is the goal of family life?" and they will unanimously answer, "To be happy." It seems as obvious as asking: "What are you breathing?" when and the answer is, "Air."

But how do we measure whether we are happy or not? The gauge is usually a bit superficial: for most of us, we are "happy" if we are having "fun." Laughter, parties, smiles, feeling good, dabbling in hobbies and diversions: this is American-style "happiness." But to such "happy" people Jesus does not say, "Blessed are you because you are happy." In future chapters will we investigate happiness and blessedness in more detail, but let us be sure that Jesus is not a peddler in the mall pitching some gimmick that will help you to be "happy."

Magical States of Grace

If blessedness is in some way about the good life, society sets us on a few other wild-goose chases. Jesus did not say,

Blessed are the cool.

In modern culture, "coolness" is what David Brooks has called "a magical state of grace."[4] Even Christians stumble into measuring how hip, how stylish and fashionable, how "in" they are, forgetting that Jesus, if anything, thrusts you off the glitzy runway and into a corner that the cool will regard as comical or pathetically dorky.

In a world where appearances are everything, notice Jesus did not say,

Blessed are the good-looking, for they will find plenty of friends.

Magazines that target teenage girls do not advise them on how to be good, or how to be smart; the readers are told that it's all about appearances, the curve of your body, the curl of your bleached hair. Boys are praised for their vertical leap or for owning a fast car.

And if we glance at what the cool stay busy doing, we must notice that Jesus did not say,

Blessed are the sexually active.

In our culture, the sexually active seem to be the happiest and most blessed of all people, since happy equals fun, and sex catapults itself to the top of the heap as the most fun possible. Nothing could be more tragic, or further removed from the mood of Jesus when he spoke the Beatitudes.

Right on the heels of the Beatitudes, Jesus turns to the subject of adultery; he pokes down into the marrow of our dark minds, equating "lust" with "adultery." Would that today we merely suffered lust. Lust is now licensed for action. Someone called it the "McDonaldization of sex": it's like fast food—no big deal. David Brooks trenchantly described life for the young nowadays, who "have no time for serious relationships. They are more likely to go out in groups—and then they hook up for occasional sex." Students he interviewed spoke of having sex "in the tone one might use to describe commuting routes," as the young glibly speak of "buddy sex" among students who distinguish "friendships" from "friendships with privileges."[5] More than half of the eleventh-graders had had sex with a casual acquaintance.

Middle-aged adults seem equally unable to restrain themselves; marriages bust up (or live on) in the face of what we once called "adultery." Turn on the television: a woman gets physical with ten different guys, then picks the one she likes the most—or a guy does the same with ten women. Teenagers and grownups who are *not* sexually active look at themselves and ask, "What is wrong with me? Am I ugly?" We should blush in embarrassment, for our sexual mores basically indicate we are no better than orangutans or rabbits—we simply *must* satisfy our desires.

But Jesus did not say,

Blessed are those who satisfy their desires.

Jesus lifts our gaze to something higher, to something more precious, more fulfilling, something enduring. After all, in the world's conventional wisdom, who gives (or doesn't give) approval? For the cool, the popular, the good-looking, and the sexually active, approval and a sense of worth rest in the eye of the beholder. Don't we let other people determine our worth? Isn't what others think of me paramount? √

"These [people] who have turned the world upside down have come here also!" The world, in which I stupidly let any- and everybody out there set my value, is hoisted up on Jesus' shoulder, turned on its head, and shaken firmly. In the kingdom of God, up is down, poor is rich, ugly is beautiful, unpopular is in, in is out, abstention is satisfaction, awkward is admirable. The approval that matters, the value that counts, is in the eyes and heart of God.

To think of this upside-downness from another angle, let us look at what the church has taught for centuries as the "seven deadly sins": lust, greed, gluttony, envy, anger, pride, and sloth. Once upon a time, these drove Christians to the confessional booth. But now, don't they describe the good life in America? Watch television, listen to chitchat in the hallway, analyze your checkbook. We are all about lust, greed, gluttony, envy, anger, pride, and sloth, and people who are facile in at least five or six out of the seven seem to have solved the riddle of life. But Jesus never says,

> *Blessed are the greedy*
> or
> *Blessed are the gluttonous* (feasting in grand restaurants or on imported wine?)
> or
> *Blessed are the envious, or the angry, or the prideful*
> or
> *Blessed are the slothful.*

Apparently, unless our argument from silence is totally misguided, Jesus still regards the seven deadly sins as *deadly*.

Sowing a Long-Term Moral Revolution

But we need to be careful, and not make Jesus sound like a stick-in-the-mud, some vapid party pooper who can't bear having a good time. What else did Jesus not say? A late-second-century religious book that was too late and too far-fetched to make it into the canon of the Bible, the "Acts of Paul and Thekla," contains these Beatitudes:

> *Blessed are the pure in heart, for they will see God.*
> *Blessed are those who have kept the flesh chaste, for they will become a temple of God.*

Blessed are those who are self-controlled, for God will speak to them.

Blessed are those who have wives as if they did not have them, for they will be the heirs of God.

Blessed are the bodies of the virgins, for these will be pleasing to God and will not lose the reward for their chastity.[6]

Self-control is a good thing, and chastity and virginity are woefully underrated in our culture.

But Jesus is not an ascetic. He is not campaigning for us to be miserable, never enjoying life. In fact, Jesus wants deeper pleasures for us, a higher enjoyment and delight in life. C. S. Lewis, back in 1941, preached an eloquent sermon, "The Weight of Glory." While people in our day may think of "unselfishness" as the highest virtue, the great Christians of old would have ranked "love" as the zenith of the virtues. We have substituted a negative, assuming somehow that desires should be denied, smothered, cooled. Then Lewis adds:

Indeed, if we consider the unblushing promises of reward and the staggering nature of the rewards promised in the Gospels, it would seem that Our Lord finds our desires not too strong, but too weak. We are half-hearted creatures, fooling about with drink and sex and ambition when infinite joy is offered us, like an ignorant child who wants to go on making mud pies in a slum because he cannot imagine what is meant by the offer of a holiday at the sea. We are far too easily pleased.[7]

Lewis is expounding that great verse from 2 Corinthians 4:17, where Paul tantalizes us: "For this slight momentary affliction is preparing for us an eternal weight of glory beyond all comparison," a text that puts the finishing touches on the beautiful portrait of life with God whose initial brushstrokes were the Beatitudes.

Even non-Christian and totally secular thinkers are onto the lie of our Madison Avenue–driven consumer culture, and understand that our cravings point to something far deeper. Marketing titillates us with perfectly shaped people with flawless skin and richly textured hair, adorned with outrageously expensive baubles; but why do we fall for it? Isn't David Brooks right?

Why do we torture ourselves with things we don't have and aren't likely to get? Why do we eagerly seek out images of lives we are unlikely to lead? It is precisely because fantasy, imagination, and dreaming play a far more significant role in our psychological makeup than we are accustomed to acknowledging. We are influenced, far more than most of us admit, by some longing for completion, some impulse toward heaven. The magazines are not really about hedonism. . . . They're not even mainly about consumption. These magazines are about aspiration.[8]

Jesus is not anti-aspiration. Jesus opens his teaching ministry with the Beatitudes not to douse cold water on our desires, but to whet our appetites, to heighten our desire, to stir in us a not-to-be-denied determination to be only the very best we can be (or rather, the very best we were made to be), to excite our imagination, to appeal to our longing for completion, to invite us to heaven.

To discern the plot of Jesus' story, to "get it," to let our mental map be crumpled up and then smoothed back out in Jesus' upside-down way of giving directions, we will need to be suspicious of the banter we overhear day in and day out. We need to be prepared for Jesus' words to take quite a long time to have their way with us, much less with anybody else out there. Archbishop Oscar Romero understood this challenge in a sermon he preached in El Salvador while being harassed by government henchmen who eventually assassinated him a year later:

The world does not say: blessed are the poor. The world says: blessed are the rich. You are worth as much as you have. But Christ says: wrong. Blessed are the poor . . . because they do not put their trust in what is so transitory. Blessed are the poor, for they know their riches are in the One who being rich made himself poor in order to enrich us with his poverty, teaching us the Christian's true wisdom.

The Beatitudes are not something we can understand fully, and that is why there are young people especially who think that the love of the Beatitudes is not going to bring about a better world and who opt for violence, for guerilla war, for revolution. The church will never make that its path. Let it be clear, I repeat, that the church does not choose those ways of violence and that whatever is said to that effect is slander. The church's option is for what Christ says in the Beatitudes. I am not surprised, though, that this is not understood. Young people especially are impatient and want a better world right away. But Christ, who preached this message twenty centuries ago, knew that he was sowing a long-term moral revolution in which we human beings come to change ourselves from worldly thinking.[9]

Questions for Discussion

1. Why do you think the Beatitudes have become part of "conventional wisdom" instead of morally revolutionary?
2. Which Beatitudes do you think are the most susceptible to being misused in today's culture?
3. In what ways do you think the church and Christians can capture the revolutionary meanings of the Beatitudes?

What Jesus Did Say

So if Jesus *didn't* say certain things, what exactly *did* Jesus say? And *where* did he say what he said? And *to whom*? In Matthew's story, Jesus has been zigzagging around the countryside that hugs the Sea of Galilee, crowds buzzing with excitement, the turnout mounting, rumors about him flying wildly.[1] Sensing we may need to pause and catch our breath as we try to keep up with this intrepid Jesus who seems in a hurry to do good, Matthew halts the action and we get to overhear what this Jesus, seated on a mountain, has to say.

> *Blessed are the poor in spirit, for theirs is the kingdom of heaven.*
> *Blessed are those who mourn, for they shall be comforted.*
> *Blessed are the meek, for they shall inherit the earth.*
> *Blessed are those who hunger and thirst for righteousness, for they shall be satisfied.*
> *Blessed are the merciful, for they shall obtain mercy.*
> *Blessed are the pure in heart, for they shall see God.*
> *Blessed are the peacemakers, for they shall be called sons of God.*
> *Blessed are those who are persecuted for righteousness' sake, for theirs is the kingdom of heaven.*
> *Blessed are you when men revile you and persecute you and utter all kinds of evil against you falsely on my account. Rejoice and be glad, for your reward is great in heaven, for so men persecuted the prophets who were before you.*
>
> (Matt. 5:3–12)

Before turning to questions like *where* and *to whom* Jesus said these things, take some time to reflect on them, to read and reread, letting the words dance in your imagination. Say the words out loud. Whisper them. At least for the season in which you are reading this book, treat them the way Jesus, from childhood to the last week of his life, treated the Jewish daily prayer, the Shema:

> These words which I command you this day shall be upon your hearts; and you shall teach them diligently to your children, and shall talk of them when you sit in your house, and when you walk by the way, and when you lie down, and when you rise. And you shall bind them as a sign upon your hand, and they shall be as frontlets between your eyes. And you shall write them on the doorposts of your house and on your gates. (Deut. 6:6–9)

Print them out and stick them on your refrigerator, or paste them in as your computer wallpaper. One of the most humble, faithful church members I have ever known had them cross-stitched and hung in a prominent spot in his bedroom. Memorize them. Sing them! An increasingly popular musical setting of the Beatitudes is David Haas's "Blest Are They." The repetition of the words, lingering over them, stumbling upon them in your desk drawer in the middle of a hectic day, letting them elicit a glance in the kitchen when you're about to raise your voice in frustration: God's transformation of your mind and life require some time, so let the Beatitudes take their time with you.

More Beatitudes?

Interestingly, the Beatitudes of Matthew 5 are not the only set of Beatitudes ever pieced together, even from Jesus. In Luke 6, Jesus (standing this time on a "level place" instead of a mountain; v.17) voices some of the same Beatitudes we have here, but in slightly different form, in a very different order. He seems a bit more direct, more blunt, perhaps with a little more fiery zeal than in Matthew 5:

> *Blessed are you poor, for yours is the kingdom of God.*
> *Blessed are you that hunger now, for you shall be satisfied.*
> *Blessed are you that weep now, for you shall laugh.*

> *Blessed are you when men hate you, and when they exclude*
> *you and revile you, and cast out your name as evil, on*
> *account of the Son of man!*
> *Rejoice in that day, and leap for joy, for behold, your reward*
> *is great in heaven; for so their fathers did to the prophets.*
> *But woe to you that are rich, for you have received your con-*
> *solation.*
> *Woe to you that are full now, for you shall hunger.*
> *Woe to you that laugh now, for you shall mourn and weep.*
> *Woe to you, when all men speak well of you, for so their*
> *fathers did to the false prophets.*
>
> (Luke 6:20–26)

We may wish he had stuck to a series of "Blessed are those that . . ." statements, instead of adding the less polite refrain of "Woe to you that. . ." Joel Green dubbed these "anti-beatitudes,"[2] and a good conversation starter might be whether Luke (with some Woe!) or Matthew (with only Blessed!) is more helpful. We will look closely at these divergences later. But for now we should ask: Why does the Bible provide us with *two* sets of Beatitudes that are far from identical? What did Jesus *really* say?

Jesus taught many times, in many places, and to many people. Like any good teacher, he reiterated certain themes, with a different spin, depending on the crowd at hand. So we need not be surprised that we have multiple versions of what Jesus said. How intriguing is it to consider that Jesus uttered Beatitudes in many villages, in several synagogues, and probably one on one with some Gentile on the road, with Peter, with John, with his mother? All we have now (really the treasure we have now) is the way Matthew retold what he had heard of it a few decades later, and the way Luke retold what he had heard of it from still others.

Outside the Scriptures of the church, the Gospel of Thomas, which was too late and did not command enough authority to be included in the Bible, passed along still different Beatitudes as coming from Jesus, such as:

> *Blessed are the hungry, for the belly of him who desires shall be*
> *filled*

and

> *Blessed are those who have been persecuted in their heart, for*
> *they have known the Father in truth.*[3]

Archaeologists have found a tiny papyrus fragment among the Dead
Sea Scrolls with some beatitudes that Jesus might have picked up in
his studies:

> *Blessed are those who babble not about paths of iniquity.*
> *Blessed is the man who has attained wisdom and walks by the*
> *law of the Most High and fixes his heart on her ways, who*
> *delights in her chastisements.*[4]

Beatitudes, sentences of blessedness, had been around a long time.
When Jesus taught, the language of the Psalms (the prayerbook of his
childhood and of all the people of Israel) fired his own imagination:

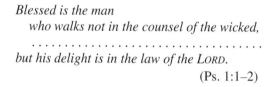

> *Blessed is the man*
> *who walks not in the counsel of the wicked,*
> . . . .
> *but his delight is in the law of the LORD.*
>   (Ps. 1:1–2)

In this book, we will focus on Matthew, given its greater familiarity,
but draw in Luke's more prickly version as we move along. So, where
did Jesus say what he said? And to whom did he say such things?

> Seeing the crowds, he went up on the mountain and when he sat
> down his disciples came to him. (Matt. 5:1)

Which mountain? We do not know precisely. But if we are familiar with the Bible, our memory ricochets back through its pages until
we get to Mount Sinai, where the people of Israel, still in the thrall of
being miraculously set free from slavery under Egypt's Pharaoh, gathered to hear what Moses brought down from God. Jesus is not on
Mount Sinai, but we are probably meant to hear an echo of the authoritative word Moses delivered to the people of Israel. Jesus is on a less
impressive mountain, more of a "hill"—for in the region of Galilee,

there are no towering "mountains." Today, above the village of Tabgha, a copper-domed church (built in 1937) is situated on a lovely slope, and the Beatitudes are etched on the sanctuary's walls; tour groups pause there to hear Jesus' words, which may well have been spoken near this place.

To whom was Jesus talking two thousand years ago? The crowds? Or just the disciples? When Luke passes along his version of the Beatitudes, the disciples are singled out: "He fixed his eyes on his disciples, and said . . ." (Luke 6:20, au. trans.). In Matthew, the disciples come, but Jesus is saying what he's saying because the "crowds" have thronged to him. Perhaps we should imagine concentric circles[5] of people listening to Jesus: the disciples close enough to reach out and touch him, then dozens or hundreds of others in the crowd, pressing, straining to hear. And who is in a third circle, but you and I—overhearing this teaching moment, with Jesus' eyes just as fixed on us as on the disciples?

The Beatitudes as a Ladder, a Staircase

What then do we hear Jesus say? Beginning in chapter 5, we will go through each Beatitude, focusing on the words, original meanings, translations. As we proceed, though, we need to be on the lookout for the "inner logic" connecting all eight Beatitudes. In his insightful discussion of the Apostles' Creed, Nicholas Lash reminds us that "words take meaning from the company they keep."[6] If we pick out a single Beatitude, forgetting the company it keeps, it could be like noticing and yanking out a loose thread, unraveling the fabric, forgetting that each thread is woven into a larger cloth with its own beauty.

Or to shift the image a bit: Jim Forest wrote an inspiring book entitled *The Ladder of the Beatitudes*, showing how each "Blessed are those who . . ." leads to the next, how they depend on each other.[7] At least as far back as the fourth century, theologians (such as Gregory of Nyssa) imagined the complete set of Beatitudes as a staircase, ascending toward God. For Jesus, the eight Beatitudes are not like the high school quiz in which "only four of these eight need be attempted in the allotted time." We will see how the poor in spirit are compelled to mourn, how the meek hunger for righteousness, how the pure in heart are merciful, and therefore they strive to make peace, and wind up being hassled because of it. And as we will see in chapter 3, the Beatitudes keep company not only with each other, but with the broader scope of Jesus' teaching, not to mention the drama of his life, death, and resurrection.

As we examine the staircase, the ladder of the Beatitudes, as we linger on each step, each rung, we notice the pointed drama in Jesus' words. This teaching is not a long, rambling tirade. Each sentence is compact, a swift plunge. Jesus is a bit of a poet here, a quotable sage. His words are pithy, flashing a rhetorical flair that should startle us a bit. Each Beatitude is jam-packed, not bothering to explain everything, inviting the listener to jot it down, to poke around inside, to ask questions, to talk with your friends and neighbors about the implications. Good teaching is like that: tossing out a pearl of an idea so shimmering with possible meaning that the student can spend a lifetime delving into the depths of truth.

And yet as we examine each pearl, dumbfounded, we remember how each pearl finds its place when strung together into the lovely necklace. Frederick Buechner, with his usual eloquence, captures the wonder of the Beatitudes taken as a whole, and what was no doubt their startling impact on the first listeners:

> Whom did Jesus single out for special commendation?
>
> Not the spiritual giants but "the poor in spirit" as he called them, the ones who spiritually speaking have absolutely nothing to give and absolutely everything to receive like the Prodigal telling his father "I am not worthy to be called thy son" only to discover for the first time all he had in having a father.
>
> Not the champions of faith who can rejoice even in the midst of suffering but the ones who mourn over their own suffering because they know for the most part they've brought it down on themselves, and over the suffering of others because that's just the way it makes them feel to be in the same room with them.
>
> Not the strong ones but the meek ones in the sense of the gentle ones. . . .
>
> Not the ones who are righteous but the ones who hope they will be someday and in the meantime are well aware that the distance they still have to go is even greater than the distance they've already come.

Not the winners of great victories over Evil in the world but the ones who, seeing it also in themselves every time they comb their hair, are merciful when they find it in others and maybe that way win the greater victory.

Not the totally pure but the "pure in heart," the ones who may be as shop-worn and clay-footed as the next one but have somehow kept some inner freshness and innocence intact.

Not the ones who have necessarily found peace in its fullness but the ones who, just for that reason, try to bring it about wherever and however they can. . . .

Jesus saved for last the ones who side with Heaven even when any fool can see it's the losing side and all you get for your pains is pain. Looking into the faces of his listeners, he speaks to them directly for the first time. "Blessed are you," he says.

You can see them looking back at him. They're not a high-class crowd—peasants and fisherfolks for the most part, on the shabby side, not all that bright. It doesn't look as if there's a hero among them. They have their jaws set, their brows furrowed with concentration.[8]

To probe the Beatitudes, we too will need to concentrate. But before we explore each rung of the letter one by one, we need to pause and reflect on a crucial issue: Does it matter who said these words?

Questions for Discussion

1. In what ways are we enriched by the two versions of the Beatitudes—in Matthew's and Luke's Gospels?
2. What interconnections do you see in the Beatitudes as each stands in relation to the others?
3. In what ways did Jesus himself embody each of the Beatitudes?

3

Why It Matters Who Said These Words

*T*he most important thing about the Beatitudes is not our analysis of the words, what they mean, whether they make sense, or if they stand a chance of survival in the marketplace of ideas. All that matters, before we've read them or after we've dissected them over a lifetime, is *who* said these words. The fact that it was Jesus who spoke them, and not only spoke them but embodied them all, compels us to revamp the way we usually hear and respond to thoughts, sayings, quotations.

Bookstores sell thick compendiums of wisdom—memorable phrases from Dickens, Dickinson, Tolstoy, Eliot, Chesterton, Sayers, Confucius, the Dalai Lama, Dylan, Angelou. But who were (or are) these people? The way we often corral wisdom is a bit like fantasy football: you grab a phrase from this person, a clever tidbit from that person, mix in a little humor from another person, and you have . . . Well, what do you have?

Sayings frequently are severed from the speaker and live out there somewhere. A given saying becomes a free-floating piece that we like or don't like, depending on whether—well, on whether we like or don't like the saying. Posters bear a kind of wisdom: Make love, not war. Regime change begins at home. Not all who wander are lost. Today is a gift; that's why they call it the present. Love makes the world go round. If you can dream it, you can do it. Who said these things? And to whom?

Does it matter? Mother Teresa said, "My secret is a very simple one: I pray." But the nuance is entirely different if George Bush said this on election night, or if Madonna said the same thing after a record went platinum. Martin Luther King Jr. said,

"I've seen the promised land," but the words would rattle a bit differently if Hugh Hefner or Arnold Schwarzenegger said the same thing.

We even suffer a confusion about who said what. I heard a talk in which the speaker began, "Emily Dickinson once wrote, 'The unknown is the mind's greatest gift, and for it no one thinks to thank God.'" I scribbled that down immediately. When I got home, I thumbed through a little collection of Dickinson poems and didn't see it. So I e-mailed the speaker, who said she had read the quotation in a book by William Sloane Coffin. So I found the Coffin book, and sure enough, Coffin quotes Emily Dickinson.[1] But in a fit of insecurity, and needing a footnote for a book I was writing, I plunged into the depths of the Duke University library and found an "exhaustive concordance" of the letters and poems of Emily Dickinson. Nothing. If she said it, it was obscure enough to miss the exhaustive concordance. So, who said this? and why did Coffin think Dickinson said it?

But does it matter? Such a great thought: I don't really care who said it, except out of a desire to defend myself to my publisher, or to appear to be well-read. How many talkers have confidently quoted Lord Acton to the effect that "Power corrupts; absolute power corrupts absolutely." Who was Lord Acton? And where, why, and to whom did he say such a thing? And was that really an original idea? Does anyone care?

The Union of Words and Person

Yet I find myself caring. I read a neighboring church's newsletter about fifteen years ago, and it quoted Flannery O'Connor: "You shall know the truth, and the truth shall make you odd." That's a good one—but again, digging about in concordances and consulting with a couple of brilliant experts on O'Connor's works turned up no indication that she actually said such a thing. But she would be the perfect speaker of such words, wouldn't she? If Timothy McVeigh or David Koresh said, "You shall know the truth, and the truth shall make you odd," the connotation is self-serving, even evil.

If some anonymous thinker said, "Love is the only power capable of turning an enemy into a friend,"[2] we may be mildly interested; but if (as is the case) Martin Luther King Jr. said this in the thick of nonviolent protests during the civil rights movement, the words carry a profound depth and peculiar challenge, because Dr. King actually loved his enemies and brought real change and reconciliation. If some anonymous soul said, "Since when are *words* the only acceptable form of prayer?" we might think we're overhearing a secular liberal who does not grasp the wonders of prayer; but if (as is the case) the speaker is Dorothy Day,[3] who not only championed the poor but also filled her days with constant prayer, we see that perhaps prayer is not an isolated act, but is a lifestyle that is embodied not merely in words but also in deeds.

So we can see the danger in separating words from their authors. What if we fail to consider the speaker of the Beatitudes? It would be easy to dismiss several of them without a moment's hesitation. "Blessed are the meek." Obviously they don't seem very blessed, so let's jettison that one. "Blessed are the poor." Hardly. "Blessed are the pure in heart." Well, nobody is really pure in heart, right? "Blessed are those who mourn." We love them, but how can they be thought of as blessed? So we dice and carve, whittling the Beatitudes down to the three or four that make sense.

But not only are the Beatitudes a set, a ladder, a stairway, woven together like threads in a rug. The Beatitudes are spoken by Jesus. Ulrich Luz reminds us that

> The Sermon on the Mount is *Jesus'* sermon: in it Jesus the Son of God speaks, through whom God guarantees the truth of his claim. An interpretation which . . . wants to be true, intelligible, or "rational" in itself is a misunderstanding.[4]

The Beatitudes are not generalized, abstract sayings, whose wisdom we debate. Jesus is the speaker: he has been healing the people, and is headed to the cross. Jesus is the embodiment of all the Beatitudes—so they become an invitation to follow, to become part of this new family of God. So the Beatitudes stretch our imaginations, as a multipaned window through which we get a glimpse of what life in proximity to Jesus is like.

When Jesus spoke, he did not think of it as an audition in which he aims to please so we will let him keep talking on the stage of our lives. We are the ones auditioning! And yet Jesus left us some space (didn't he?), not overwhelming us with the unbearable force of his words, but asking questions, teasing us into a new perspective, allowing us to stick around, luring us to hang close. The closer we live to Jesus, the more Jesus is on our minds, the more we will understand the Beatitudes.

The Beatitudes in the Beauty of the Gospel

Matthew frames the "authority" of Jesus who speaks these Beatitudes in several ways. The Gospel opens with a genealogy that invokes a royal, messianic lineage. The narrative of Jesus' birth chalks his entire existence up to something ineffably greater than human initiative. Jesus submits to the baptism of John, and the Spirit descends on him like a dove. He survives the devil's daunting test in the wilderness, and then appears on the mountain virtually as another Moses. And Jesus did not talk for a while and then head back to the comforts of home. He pressed into perilous zones, touching the untouchables, rocking sensibilities, to the point that even the religious leaders wished him dead—and acted on those wishes. How eerie, though: for when he breathed his last, the curtain of the temple ripped, the ground shook, and graves opened, and the speaker of the Beatitudes didn't stay dead in the grave the way even the wisest, most revered teachers tended to do.[5]

Jesus, we may then say, has "authority." Yet, authority is problematical nowadays. Authority is everywhere and rightfully questioned; we find it difficult to settle on where authority rests (if anywhere). Even if we think of the Bible (or Jesus himself) as having authority, issues of how to interpret what is authoritative befuddle us. Authority can be crushing, belittling, squelching whatever chance there might be for freedom, growth, and creativity.

Even granting a healthy hesitation to think of Jesus as authoritative, we can observe the peculiar *way* Jesus presented himself. Jesus did not marshal an array of rational arguments that forced assent. Jesus did not shout down all naysayers and leave them at a loss for words. Jesus left himself wide-open for criticism. He watched as some people waved his words off as nonsense, although others were intrigued. His strategy seemed to be to have no strategy. He simply lived, and spoke, and listeners to this day can do with him as they will.

Perhaps when we think of Jesus, and especially his Beatitudes, we might consider the *beauty* of Jesus, his story, and his words, and imagine these images of blessedness as a painting, or a symphony, or a ballet—a work of art that draws us in, that evokes desire, that sweeps us up in the movement of words that are not merely words but the brushstrokes, the harmony, the grace of God's new way in the world.

Trusting that beauty, looking for that beauty, may be the way forward in a world where "the center does not hold." Early in his ministry, Martin Luther King Jr. preached a sermon entitled "How the Christian Overcomes Evil," which featured an illustration from mythology. At the passage between Scylla and Charybdis, sirens with their seductive songs repeatedly lured sailors into shipwreck. Ulysses coped with this by stopping up the ears of his rowers with wax, and strapping himself to the mast of the ship. Christians may stake themselves on the authority of Scripture or try to shut out competing voices. But a better way to think about countering evil would be to recall Orpheus. When approaching the rocks of disaster, Orpheus simply pulled out his lyre and played an even more beautiful song, so his rowers listened to him and did not notice the sirens.[6]

To a beleaguered people in ancient times, and to a hollow people in modern times, Jesus sat down and played so our open ears might hear his marvelous music: "Blessed are the poor in spirit . . . Blessed are those who mourn . . . Blessed are the meek"—and so the singer ascended the scale, a simple melody joined by haunting harmonies. The Beatitudes are an overture to the symphony of Jesus' teaching. Chords and melodies are voiced that will resound throughout Matthew and our other Gospels.

The Beatitudes as Autobiographical

Then too, not only did Jesus talk about meekness, poverty of spirit, peacemaking, and mercy; he *was* meek, merciful, poor, and finally persecuted and reviled. When reading the Beatitudes, we may overhear something of an autobiographical reflection, as if Jesus is saying in a subtext, "This is who I am, and so this is what friendship with me looks like, for this is what oneness with God looks like."

Blessed are the poor. To a would-be follower, Jesus said, "Foxes have holes, and birds of the air have nests; but the Son of man has nowhere to lay his head" (Matt. 8:20). Jesus was born in a stable, and fled as a refugee to Egypt. His first sermon in his backwater home-town proclaimed good news to the poor, and he always expressed special affection for those who, like himself, owned nothing. He lived off the hospitality of others, and rode a donkey instead of a warhorse. His execution was the kind reserved for slaves and nobodies. What greater poverty could be imagined than for God's own Son to come down from heaven and take on humanity?

> Have this mind among yourselves, which is yours in Christ Jesus, who, though he was in the form of God, did not count equality with God a thing to be grasped, but emptied himself, taking the form of a servant, . . . he humbled himself and became obedient unto death, even death on a cross. Therefore God has highly exalted him. (Phil. 2:5–9)

Blessed are the poor in spirit, for theirs is the kingdom of heaven. The devil had offered Jesus dominion over "all the kingdoms of the world," but Jesus preferred poverty, for nothing consumed him but the kingdom of heaven.

The devil also had offered Jesus food. But this Jesus did not live "by bread alone, but by every word that proceeds from the mouth of God" (Matt. 4:4). *Blessed are those who hunger and thirst for righteousness.* At the beginning of his ministry, Jesus fasted; and at the end, just before he breathed his last, Jesus thirsted. The Samaritan woman drew water at the well, but Jesus talked about "living water": "Whoever drinks of the water that I shall give him will never thirst; the water that I shall give him will become in him a spring of water welling up to eternal life" (John 4:13–14). The disciples worried that Jesus wasn't eating enough; but to their pleas that he eat, Jesus said, "My food is to do the will of him who sent me, and to accomplish his work" (John 4:34). Did Jesus not confirm the truth of *Blessed are those who hunger and thirst for righteousness, for they shall be satisfied*? And isn't the righteousness that satisfies our deepest hunger nothing but Christ himself?

Blessed are the pure in heart. When Jesus taught at the home of Mary and Martha, he chided Martha and praised Mary, saying, "One thing is needful" (Luke 10:42). For he knew that one thing. When Jesus exposed the heart of adultery as lust, and the heart of killing as anger, he was pleading for a purity of heart that was not unfamiliar to himself. When

Jesus prayed in Gethsemane, "Not my will, but your will be done" (Matt. 26:39, au. trans.), he was only consummating what he had practiced throughout his lifetime of prayer and availability to the God he saw so clearly. *Blessed are the pure in heart, for they will see God.*

Blessed are the merciful. Jesus not only spoke compellingly about mercy in his teaching, as in the parable of the settling of accounts (Matt. 18:21–35) or in his vision of the sheep and goats (Matt. 25:31–46). Jesus was abundantly merciful to people who knew no mercy at all: lepers, demoniacs, tax collectors. Jesus' ears were specially tuned to those who cried out for mercy (Matt. 9:27). Aren't his best stories, of the Prodigal Son and the Good Samaritan, all about the mercy that Jesus himself was? When the woman caught in adultery was brought to him, Jesus drew in the sand and sent those who would stone her on their way (John 8:1–11).

Blessed are the meek. Jesus, obviously not employing the methodologies of how to gather a powerful, influential following, revealed himself by saying, "I am gentle and lowly in heart" (Matt. 11:29). Hauled before Pontius Pilate, Jesus was not belligerent or defensive; he did not bolt and run, but stood "like a lamb that is led to the slaughter" (Isa. 53:7), and said nothing. The night before, when the disciples were elbowing for the best seats, Jesus was merciful and meek, rising from the table to deal with them, using a basin and towel, washing their feet as a base servant might do (John 13:1–17).

So Jesus was not just talking or wishing when he said, *Blessed are the peacemakers.* Jesus never tired in his labor for reconciliation. He taught this incessantly, of course, that we should make peace before coming to the altar, that we should forgive as we ask for forgiveness, that we should love our enemies (Matt. 5:23–47). These were not mere words: Jesus loved his enemies. Mind you, he *made* enemies, but he loved them, and made peace with them. While enduring the gruesome agonies of crucifixion, Jesus looked down at the perpetrators and prayed, "Father, forgive them" (Luke 23:34). The night before he died, Jesus said, "Peace I leave with you; my peace I give to you; not as the world gives do I give to you" (John 14:27). The cross was the nexus of reconciliation between us and God, and Jesus was the one who could make such peace, because "He is our peace, . . . and has broken down the dividing wall of hostility" (Eph. 2:14).

Why did Jesus endure such humility, such suffering, for us? *Blessed are those who mourn.* Over and over in the Gospels, when Jesus saw the crowds, he was "moved." The Greek word, *splangnizomai*, means something like "his gut wrenched." Jesus surveyed the holy city of Jerusalem, and the throngs gathered for the great Passover festival, and he wept over the city (Luke 19:41). After his dear friend Lazarus died, Jesus arrived in Bethany, and instead of calmly raising a scepter-like hand of authority, he did what only the most beautiful Savior could do: "Jesus wept" (John 11:35, the shortest verse of the entire Bible, a flawless little jewel that refracts the full glory of God in just two small words). In Gethsemane, Jesus sobbed with a frightening, yet inviting intensity.

When Jesus said, "Blessed are those who mourn," he stood on a hill, and when his own mourning ultimately embodied itself, he was lifted up "on a hill far away." Jesus was taunted, mocked, insulted, and deserted—an incongruous fate for this one who was poor, meek, pure, peaceful, and merciful. Yet hidden in the unprecedented injustice of that old rugged cross is the truth of the Beatitudes: *Blessed are those who are persecuted . . . Blessed are you when men revile you, . . . and utter all kinds of evil against you falsely. . . . Rejoice and be glad.* Gregory of Nyssa asked what our reward would be for being persecuted for Christ:

> What is it that we will obtain? What is the prize? What is the crown? It seems to me that for which we hope is nothing other than the Lord himself. He is . . . the crown of those who win. He is the one who distributes the inheritance, he himself is the good inheritance. He is the good portion and the giver of the portion, he is the one who makes rich and is himself the riches.[7]

Rejoice and be glad! And so we can, because it matters who said these words.

Questions for Discussion

1. Do you believe it matters that the Beatitudes were given to us by Jesus and not by someone else? Why or why not?

2. In what ways do the Beatitudes have "authority" for us because they were uttered by Jesus?

3. Do the Beatitudes become more meaningful when we link them to Jesus' own life and ministry? Why is this important?

Blessed

*A*nd so we begin, one step at a time, to progress upward toward God on the staircase of the Beatitudes.

He opened his mouth and taught them, saying, "Blessed are. . . ." (Matt. 5:2–3)

When Jesus opened his mouth, he spoke in Aramaic. Since Matthew wrote his story in Greek, any English translation is actually two languages removed from Jesus' original words! The Greek word we frequently render as "blessed" is *makarios*. Back in chapter 1, we noted that many commentators have anointed "happy" as the best translation of *makarios*, and that Robert Schuller's cleverly titled *The Be Happy Attitudes* has been a bestseller. The translation itself is not wrong, but we need to beware: ancient people did not harbor a superficial, "fun"-oriented view of happiness, or of being blessed. Robert Wilken summarizes the difference:

> For us the term *happiness* has come to mean "feeling good" or enjoying certain pleasures, a transient state that arrives and departs as circumstances change or fortune intervenes. For the ancients, happiness was a possession of the soul, something that one acquired and that, once acquired, could not easily be taken away. Happiness designated the supreme aim of human life . . . living in accord with nature, in harmony with our deepest aspirations as human beings.[1]

Many Americans hear the word "happy" very differently. We fancy the notion of Jesus smiling and providing tips on "how to be happy," and would be disappointed should Jesus not give us a boost in our very Americanized "pursuit of happiness." But as you have pondered the Beatitudes, you may have noticed a couple of problems. Those who are poor, who mourn, who are meek, and who are persecuted and reviled don't sound very "happy," do they? And if it is true that we identify happiness with "fun" (Are my children happy? = Are my children having fun? Is my marriage happy? = Are we having fun?), then doesn't the very question "Am I happy?" derail us from Jesus' path? "Am I happy?" asks about *me*, and turns me in on myself; but isn't Jesus interested in us opening ourselves outward to God and to others? "Happiness" is something I pursue; happiness is up to me. But Jesus' Beatitudes are about what we cannot achieve, what we cannot make happen, what we can only receive as the most startling of gifts.

Blessedness as God's Gift

The "-*ed*" ending on the word "blessed" is a hint: there is something passive about being blessed. I am not at this moment doing any blessing myself; I am being blessed. "Blessed" is all gift. "Blessed" surprises me. If the Beatitudes hang together as a set, we might reflect on this thought from Frederick Dale Bruner: he believes the first half of the Beatitudes describe our "need" (poor, mourn, meek, hunger); the latter half describe things we do to "help" (being merciful, peacemaking, and getting harassed for trying). Whether Jesus intended this kind of artistic structure or not, Bruner's theological conclusion is on target: "God helps those who cannot help themselves (the need Beatitudes), and he also helps those who try to help others (the help Beatitudes), but he does not in any Beatitude help those who think they can help themselves."[2]

"Blessed" really means "wonderful news," and it is God's wonderful news. God is acting now through Jesus to turn the world upside down. God has come down to help those who are under no illusion that they can help themselves. So to be "blessed" isn't catchy advice on how to go and be happy; rather, "blessed" is being swept up in God's decisive movement in the world. "It's about something that's starting to happen, not about a general truth of life. It is *gospel*: good news, not good advice" (Tom Wright).[3]

Parenthetically, talk of "blessings" as "gifts" can confuse. A few years ago, shoppers snapped up millions of copies of *The Prayer of Jabez*, a book that bears more wisdom than critics like to admit. Yet in this book "blessings" get reduced to "things," and the blessings always are obviously good things. The author, Bruce Wilkinson, tells of an imaginary Mr. Jones arriving in heaven, where he is treated to a tour by (of course) St. Peter. Mr. Jones notices an enormous warehouse, but Peter hesitates to let him in. "Why would there be any secrets in heaven?" Jones wonders. "What incredible surprise could be waiting for me in there?" Finally Peter relents. Inside the warehouse, Jones eyes row after row of shelves,

> floor to ceiling, each stacked neatly with white boxes tied in red ribbons. "These boxes all have names on them," Mr. Jones muses aloud. Then turning to Peter he asks, "Do I have one?" "Yes, you do." There in Mr. Jones's white box are all the blessings that God wanted to give to him while he was on earth . . . but Mr. Jones had never asked.

Wilkinson's lesson?

> That's the catch—if you don't ask for His blessing, you forfeit those that come to you only when you ask. Your Father is delighted to respond generously when His blessing is what you covet most.[4]

The notion of a divine warehouse full of packages (for *me*!), just waiting for *me* to back my station wagon up to the door and load up by simply asking is laughably problematical. But the conclusive, eighth Beatitude might teach us that if there were boxes of blessedness to be collected, we might open them and find them to contain, not neat goodies we'd hate to miss out on, but harder realities we might prefer to leave in the bay. The saints who have lived most closely to God have opened their "boxes" and discovered that following Jesus can and does leave you marginalized, ostracized, wounded, in danger, and even dead. If we try to yank out the thread of the final Beatitudes, we unravel the fabric, and think God is boxing up a little kingdom, something comforting, even a grand inheritance—forgetting that promises are for the future, not this minute, forgetting the immense cost of discipleship.

Commandments? Or Promises?

Yet whatever the cost, following Jesus is "worth it," although, as we will see, the calculating kind of mind-set that asks questions like whether following Jesus is "worth it" misses the point, and never is embraced by blessedness. I do not strive to do the Jesus thing figuring the investment will pay off. Like a bear drawn naturally to honey, or like the infant drawn to his mother's breast, once I find myself moving toward Christ, no clever effort on my part is required. I am amazed to discover my true self; the delight of being near Christ is all gift, the promise fulfilled. The world, I now see, is not turned upside down so much as it is finally set right side up. The hidden inner secret of the universe is now out in the open.

Thinking of the Beatitudes as God's promise is liberating, and is hopeful. But doesn't Jesus really want me to *do* something—to *be* poor in spirit? and pure in heart? and to get busy with peacemaking or purity of heart? Implicitly, yes, Jesus *is* recommending a way of life, a posture we should assume, habits we should practice until they are second nature in our lives. And yet the way we think about this way of life, these habits, is tricky. Subtly I may calculate to behave a certain way to get Jesus *for me!* But "whoever would save his life will lose it" (Mark 8:35). The gift of the Beatitudes is kin to another curious thought from Jesus: "Do not let your left hand know what your right hand is doing" (Matt. 6:3). How much more wonderful is it to be drawn in, almost when we weren't looking? A promise was uttered, and in response to our good fortune we simply nodded spontaneously. If I begin to be poor in spirit or meek, if I hunger and thirst for righteousness or become more pure in heart, I am startled, and can think of nothing to say but "It is no longer I who live, but Christ who lives in me" (Gal. 2:20).

We may compare the "ethic" of the Beatitudes to the "fruit of the Spirit." Holiness is never a matter of gritting your teeth and trying really diligently to do what God requires. We may grit our teeth, and we do try hard. But I am not able to do what God wants of me; I am not capable of the life God wants for me. A changed life is the gift of God's Spirit. Paul did not speak of "the fruit of my good intentions," but "the fruit of the Spirit": "love, joy, peace, patience, kindness, goodness, faithfulness, gentleness, self-control, against such there is no law" (Gal. 5:22–23).

Not only are these not against the law. They are not the law! Paul does not say, "You must be joyful, patient, faithful." Jesus did not say, "You must be poor in spirit, meek, and merciful." Rather, if we just calm down and let the Spirit have its way with us, we discover to our delightful surprise traces of joy, peace, and gentleness, meekness, hunger for righteousness, and purity of heart in our lives, all gift, all the work of God in us. The Spirit is moving. Jesus has spoken. A window has been thrown open into God's heart, into God's future, into God's kingdom dawning even now.

We can see that the dawning of the kingdom of God is going to be far bigger than me and my spirituality. Jesus did not come to earth to dispense a few little nuggets to help me develop my spiritual self. Jesus' mission was cosmic in scope, turning history itself on its ear, transforming not just me but the universe. When Jesus sat on that mountain and told the disciples and the larger crowds, "Blessed are those who . . . ," he was describing blessedness quite simply as being near God, being in sync with God, snuggling up close to truth, committed to follow in Jesus' way, the results of which will not seem blessed at all to those who have never heard of Jesus.

In the Beatitudes, something subversive is on the loose. If Jesus is serious, he is talking about turning the world and its values upside down, about a revolutionary future where up is down, right is left, poor is rich, tears are laughter—something akin to what the wise wizard Gandalf wrote to his hobbit friend Frodo in *The Lord of the Rings*:

> All that is gold does not glitter,
> Not all those who wander are lost;
> The old that is strong does not wither,
> Deep roots are not reached by the frost.
> From the ashes a fire shall be woken,

A light from the shadows shall spring:
Renewed shall be blade that was broken,
The crownless again shall be king.[5]

Theologians call this sort of thinking "eschatological," and Jesus is even more radically futuristic than Gandalf (or any of us). For Jesus, the most real reality is not the hill where he sits or the clothes he wears or the perspiration he smells from Simon Peter standing nearby. The most palpable reality to him is the ultimate, eternal kingdom of God, which you and I cannot see just yet, which will not dawn until time has darkened, yet is more certain than the steely power of Rome or the snarling governorship of King Herod.

But we need not linger too long on the meaning of "blessed." To know what Jesus meant by being "blessed," let us grasp the first rung of the ladder, gingerly taking that first step in our ascent to togetherness with Christ.

Questions for Discussion

1. What are the differences between "Happy are. . ." and "Blessed are . . ."?
2. Why is it important to see blessedness as a divine gift?
3. What difference does it make to see the Beatitudes as "promises" instead of "commandments"?

Poor in Spirit

Blessed are the poor in spirit.

—Matthew 5:3

While a few of the wealthy elite may have been sprinkled through the crowds to whom Jesus spoke,[1] the overwhelming (and overwhelmed!) majority of people who saw and heard him were poor. Because of the economy, the cruel system of Roman taxation, and the demographics of people living off the land, clustered in tiny hamlets, the poor were everywhere, and they were the ones drawn to Jesus. The Greek word for "poor," *ptochoi*, implies that they are not merely low on funds, but miserable, oppressed, humiliated. So the miserable, oppressed, and humiliated are blessed?

To people who had no hope, who were never *in* on anything, Jesus was a breath of the freshest air. In Luke's version, Jesus launches into the Beatitudes right on the heels of a series of up-close-and-personal encounters with a leper (and no one could be more shunned than a victim of this dreaded skin disease), a paralytic, a tax collector (the scoundrels who bilked the poor of their desperately needed, hard-earned money), a man with a withered hand, and the chronically ill. Like a magnet attracting to himself the *ptochoi* who had suffered the worst, Jesus began his best sermon by declaring, "Blessed are you poor" (Luke 6:20).

At least, that's how he got rolling in Luke. Matthew adds (to the relief of many who can afford to buy books like this one) "in spirit." Blessed are the poor *in spirit*—which makes much more sense, doesn't it? What could be blessed about poverty? When

John Kennedy was running for the Senate, he was quizzed during a campaign stop by a poor laborer: "Mr. Kennedy, do you know what it's like to not be able to pay your bills, to wonder how you'll get food on the table, to struggle just to make ends meet? Do you know what it is like to be poor?" Kennedy, not even trying to pretend he was anything other than a blueblood patrician, softly answered, "No, I don't know what it's like to be poor." The man in the crowd said, "Well, you haven't missed a thing."

Jesus didn't glamorize poverty, and neither should we. But maybe when we have much, we miss lots of things. To Jesus, the Kennedys of the world, as well as the widespread majority of us who aren't downright poor, suffer a stiff disadvantage spiritually, for we are easily deluded into thinking we can manage our own world: we get what we want, and we can thank ourselves for it. We lose that sense of spiritual poverty, the sense of utter dependence upon God, a humble posture before God and others, the total openness to God, who really is all we have at the end of the day. Jim Forest said, "Being poor in spirit means letting go of the myth that the more I possess, the happier I'll be."[2]

Added to this confusion about our identity is that our very labor to flee poverty can barricade us from receiving the grace of God. Frederick Buechner painted the perfect mental image: we live our lives like a big clenched fist. The clenched fist can do many things: it can work, hang on to things, impress, even fight. But, "the one thing a clenched fist cannot do is accept, even from the good God himself, a helping hand."[3]

Spiritual Childhood

Does Jesus mean "Blessed are the poor"? Or is it merely an image, "Blessed are the poor in spirit" (Matt. 5:3)? Clarence Jordan, who read his Bible and thought he was supposed to do whatever it said, started a farm, a commune, where blacks and whites lived together, sharing their property in common—and he did this in the 1940s in rural Georgia, subjecting himself to the hatred of the KKK and affluent Georgians. Preaching on this question of whether Jesus meant spiritual poverty or monetary poverty, he said:

If you have a lot of money, you'll probably say spiritual poverty. If you have little or no money, you'll probably say physical poverty. The rich will thank God for Matthew; the poor will thank God for Luke. Who's right? Chances are, neither one. For it is exactly this attitude of self-praise and self-justification and self-satisfaction that robs men of a sense of great need for the kingdom and its blessings. When one says "I don't need to be poor in things; I'm poor in spirit," and another says "I don't need to be poor in spirit; I'm poor in things," both are justifying themselves as they are saying in unison, "I don't need." With that cry on his lips, no man can repent.[4]

Indeed. The poor in spirit, whether they are physically poor or not, are those who do not try for one second to justify themselves. They do not assert their rights, they do not puff themselves up with their poverty. They are humble, they need. Gustavo Gutiérrez calls this our "spiritual childhood,"[5] our utter dependence upon and openness to God.

Notice he said "spiritual childhood." The most menacing nemesis to our relationship with God can be our very own spirituality. As we immerse ourselves in the Bible, as prayer becomes part of our daily regimen, as we build service into our weekly routine, we begin to flex our spiritual muscle—and some bizarre amnesia blocks out the sense of poverty that drove us to read the Bible, pray, and serve in the first place. We become like the excellent man at whom Jesus poked fun, who prayed, "God, I thank thee that I am not like other men" (Luke 18:11). How humbling: when I am not looking, something pernicious attaches itself to the underside of my virtue. Isn't it good to be obedient, dutiful, hardworking, and self-sacrificing? But at the precise moment that I act generously or prayerfully, some sneaky anger, or resentment, or a judgmental spirit rears its head: why don't others do as I am doing?

Perhaps when Luke's Jesus says, "Woe to you that are rich, for you have received your consolation," we may shudder if we are the type who prefer the additional "in spirit." "Woe to the rich in spirit, for they have received their reward!" How tragic would it be if, after laboring diligently in the field of spirituality, the only reward would be so I might look at myself and pronounce this self-verdict: "How spiritual

I am! and thank God I am not like others." Or worse, that others would flatter me: "How spiritual he is!" The hard question we cannot escape as we read these Beatitudes is: "Have I already received my reward?"[6]

Clearly, for Jesus, the monetarily poor have a considerable advantage over the monetarily rich, not because money is inherently evil, but because of all the meaning society attaches to our money. We gawk at the rich, we envy the rich, we measure our worth by our investments or salary; and while we know money won't make a person happy, we suspect it couldn't hurt.

But according to Jesus, it *can* and often *does* hurt. In Luke's Beatitudes, in which Jesus turns the tables with a "Woe!" to those who are rich (Luke 6:24), we see Jesus repeatedly clanging a bell of warning, telling story after story unmasking the perils of wealth: A man tears down his barns to build bigger barns, only to lose everything (Luke 12:16–21). The rich man ignores poor, sore-covered Lazarus right outside his own doorway (Luke 16:19–31). The so-called "rich young ruler" exits the very presence of Jesus, so attached is he to his wealth (Luke 18:18–30). Clearly, if the Beatitudes are a "ladder," the rungs lead you in the opposite direction from the way our capitalist society lures you. No "upward mobility" here!

The spiritual advantage of poverty is sometimes glimpsed, in God's bizarre dispensation, when someone loses a job or suffers financial duress—or even when some other crisis forces us to discover for the first time

> the grief, the anguish of being helpless to be anything but what you were not meant to be. . . . Strangely, it is in this helplessness that we come upon the beginning of joy. This great poverty is our greatest fortune. For when we are stripped of the riches that were not ours and could not possibly endow us with anything but trouble . . . then we become aware that the whole meaning of our life is a poverty and emptiness which, far from being a defeat, are really the pledge of all the great supernatural gifts of which they are a potency. We become like vessels that have been emptied of water that they may be filled with wine. We are like glass cleansed of dust and grime to receive the sun and vanish into its light. (Thomas Merton)[7]

It is no accident that so much of Jesus' ministry was focused on poverty, and through the history of the church the greatest saints have chosen poverty, even professing that they are able to glimpse the very face of Christ in the poor. In prayer, in reflection, we contemplate our inner poverty, our mortality, our humble status before God. We seek physical proximity to the poor, serving with them, befriending them— for they remind us of our genuine poverty. Corporations and schools do lots of "charity" and "service hours" nowadays. But it is different for us. I am not a "have" dropping a few goodies down on a "have-not." I am poor, I want to be near the poor, for then I will be near Jesus, who was poor, who became poor for us. Blessed are the poor, in spirit *and* in the bank vaults. The wise know: we are mere beggars before God.

And if I let the Spirit infuse me with holy poverty, I become generous, for what once appeared to be mine isn't mine at all. In Marilynne Robinson's lovely novel *Gilead*, a man tells about his grandfather, who "never kept anything that was worth giving away, or let us keep it, either, so my mother said. He would give laundry right off the line. . . . I believe he was a saint of some kind."[8] Blessed are the poor in spirit, Jesus would say. In Jesus' upside-down view of the universe, what do the poor, who usually get nothing at all, have coming?

"Theirs Is the Kingdom of Heaven"

Hints of royalty, glory, grandeur! The poor never even dream of such! But what exactly is this "kingdom of heaven"? Scholars have put forward definitions, like "the reign of God." The kingdom of heaven is, according to W. D. Davies and Dale Allison,

> not the territory God rules or will rule—it was not just a place, like Shangra La—but God's eschatological activity as ruler. In its fullness, this rule . . . was still unrealized, and its arrival would mark the end or transformation of the world. . . . Yet God's rule was also spoken of by Jesus as already present, and this claim was distinctive.[9]

The kingdom is out in the future, but it is already present. The tension teases us, and our best read on the time frame of the kingdom is that it is dawning right now, like the sun dazzling pink on the horizon, like the crest of a wave curling over your shoulder—although the tension is never quite resolved, is it? The kingdom is dawning *now*, but wait five minutes, or five months, or five hundred years, and it's dawning *now*. On this side of eternity, the kingdom of God always has this kind of elusive presence. It's almost here, it's not quite here, it's real; yet it eludes your grasp, so tantalizingly close, but not quite here, yet close enough to feel its breath, the warmth.

Some might mistakenly infer that this elusiveness indicates the kingdom is invisible, or unreal in some way, merely "spiritual." When Matthew calls it the kingdom *of heaven*, he does not mean *not of this earth*! In the Lord's Prayer, Jesus taught us to ask, "Thy kingdom come . . . on earth as it is in heaven." The kingdom dawns, but your feet are on solid earth when the sun begins to rise; your feet feel the gritty sand as the wave laps around you. The kingdom is not invisible, but palpable, as real as the flesh of your hand noticing your pocket is empty, as tangible as an embrace, as visible as the face of Jesus.

So what exactly is this kingdom? The promised kingdom of heaven is too marvelous for any definition; it eludes analysis. Perhaps the kingdom is like a joke which, if you have to explain it, isn't funny any longer—or like a painting or symphony, whose pleasures are had in the gazing and listening, the savoring and relishing, not in defining why Mozart added an F-sharp in the oboe or how Rembrandt mixed his paints.

What is the kingdom of heaven? The answer is unfolded in the Beatitudes themselves, and in the rest of Jesus' teaching and life. All the beatitudes define the kingdom: "As a single ray of light passing through a prism is broken into the colourful spectrum of the rainbow, so too what the kingdom brings finds colourful development in the promises of the Beatitudes" (Leonhard Goppelt).[10]

The kingdom of heaven, oddly enough, is where the poor in spirit are. The kingdom is evidenced in those who hunger and thirst for righteousness, in acts of mercy, in valiant efforts at peacemaking. The kingdom inevitably is where there is opposition and ridicule. How do we define the kingdom? Jesus didn't dictate a theological dictionary: the kingdom zooms by, and if you get caught up in the vortex of the trailing winds, you hear a story about a sower, about a boy and his father, a woman who'd been sick forever, a leper nobody else would touch, a pearl dug up in a field. To understand, to experience the kingdom, you stick as closely as possible to Jesus himself. In short, the kingdom is wherever Jesus is.

The kingdom of heaven is revolutionary, for to use the word "kingdom" implies that Caesar and Rome, and their puppet client, King Herod, are usurpers, mere pretenders. In the face of the unquestionable might of the kingdom of Rome, Jesus announced the dawn of a rival kingdom, this kingdom of heaven, which would elicit little more than laughter, but which would over the centuries turn all rivals to dust.

But then, the kingdom is about the dust from which we have all come. Listen to this lyrical reflection from Frederick Buechner:

> If we only had eyes to see and ears to hear and wits to understand, we would know that the Kingdom of God in the sense of holiness, goodness, beauty is as close as breathing and is crying out to be born both within ourselves and within the world; we would know that the Kingdom of God is what we all of us hunger for above all other things even when we don't know its name or realize that it's what we're starving to death for. The Kingdom of God is where our best dreams come from and our truest prayers. We glimpse it at those moments when we find ourselves being better than we are and wiser than we know. We catch sight of it when at some moment of crisis a strength seems to come to us that is greater than our own strength. The Kingdom of God is where we belong. It is home, and whether we realize it or not, I think we are all of us homesick for it.[11]

Are you homesick? Is there a sadness in your spirit which most certainly is poor? For you, impoverished and with a longing sadness, Jesus has something else to say.

Questions for Discussion

1. What are examples of the "spiritual poverty" we all experience?
2. What is your understanding of the "kingdom of heaven" which the "poor in spirit" are promised to inherit?
3. In what sense is the kingdom of heaven a future reality? a present reality?

What do we think when we hear "mourn"?

Those Who Mourn

Blessed are those who mourn.

—Matthew 5:4

*I*n the popular film, *Four Weddings and a Funeral*, the hilarity of a band of friends was interrupted by the sudden death of Gareth. His closest companion spoke at the funeral, using W. H. Auden's moving words to suggest that in grief we "stop all the clocks, cut off the telephone . . ." and gather about the coffin.

> I thought that love would last forever. I was wrong. . . .
> For nothing now can ever come to any good.

We pity those who mourn. We avert our gaze, dash off a note, send a spray of carnations. We say a prayer, and we may even apply a theological balm of words, something like "He's in a better place." We hope the mourners "feel better" soon. We get back to the weddings and hilarity.

Around Galilee, when Jesus lived, mourning wasn't so rushed, or so hushed. Mourners would literally tear the clothes off their own backs. Right out in the open, mourners would scream out in agony, scoop up dirt in their hands and shake the dust out onto the tops of their heads. No one tried to go to work, or to "stay busy." Friends gathered, and they lingered over their grief for at least a week in this intense fashion. They pitied those who mourned.

What did Jesus say? "Blessed are those who mourn." They seem cursed to us. We want to put away the veil of mourning as quickly as possible, returning to the jovial plot line, as did Gareth's friends in the film. But perhaps you stay with someone who mourns, you listen, you stick with her, you listen to his story, you bear her tears. I know a father whose teenage daughter was killed in an accident. Everyone wanted him to "feel better," but he did not want to feel better, for a return to a "happy" life would be to forget her. To try to fill the hole she left with anything would be futile. He did not wish to banish the hurt, for he had not stopped loving.

The wisest book I have read on grief is *Lament for a Son*, written by the Yale philosopher Nicholas Wolterstorff in the aftermath of the mountain-climbing death of his twenty-five-year-old son, Eric. Several years after this horrible loss, Wolterstorff noticed that the wound "is no longer raw. But it has not disappeared. That is as it should be. If he was worth loving, he is worth grieving over. Grief is existential testimony to the worth of the one loved. . . . Every lament is a love-song."[1]

And how strange is it that, in the darkest throes of grief, people report later how palpable was their sense of God's presence? Wolterstorff, grappling after God, discovered the truer, deeper nature of God: "Through the prism of my tears I have seen a suffering God."[2] If the Beatitudes really are a ladder, then poverty of spirit is never better known than in grief. Without bothering to sign up, we find ourselves almost accidentally enrolled in the school of mourning.

Blessed are those who mourn? Does Jesus mean merely our own personal losses? What about our sins? If we read the journal entries of spiritual giants, we find women and men who contemplate their sins and shed tears of grief. Thérèse of Lisieux wept over the slightest sense of separation from Christ she felt. In the shadow of the cross of Christ, an intense mourning over the gaping hole in the soul, the yawning gap between me and God, is entirely fitting. To those who grieve over their sin, to those who lament their distance from Jesus, our Lord says, "Blessed are those who mourn." His mission was precisely to comfort sinners.

The Prism of Tears

Wolterstorff shares another probing reflection: he believed that, after the loss of his son, he would for the rest of his life look at the world "through tears. Perhaps I shall see things that dry-eyed I could not see."[3] Dry-eyed, we may look right past the pain, the loneliness, the ache the next person harbors. Dry-eyed, we may flit off to a party, forgetting that war is being waged on this planet, that children are dying during that party for simple lack of food or medicine. Dry-eyed, we forget the gross unfairness of the world's system of meting out its rewards: the evil seem to succeed, while the holy, the humble, those who look like these Beatitudes, suffer. Listen to what Wolterstorff saw through his tears:

> When you and I are left to our own devices, it's the smiling, successful ones of the world that we cheer. . . . We turn away from the crying ones of the world. Our photographers tell us to smile. "Blessed are those who mourn." What can it mean?

His answer is a window thrown open into the life of the world:

> The mourners are those who have caught a glimpse of God's new day, who ache with all their being for the day's coming, and who break out into tears when confronted with its absence. . . . The mourners are aching visionaries. Such people Jesus blessed. . . . The Stoics of antiquity said: Be calm. Disengage yourself. Jesus says: Be open to the wounds of the world. Mourn humanity's mourning, weep over humanity's weeping, be wounded by humanity's wounds, be in agony over humanity's agony. But do so in the good cheer that a day of peace is coming.[4]

The poor in spirit are uncannily able to snuggle up to the very heart of God, and we feel what God feels, we feel what God's children feel, we dwell right inside the mind, the heart of God. We see as God sees, and so we mourn, and because we mourn as God mourns, Jesus declares us "blessed." Richard Rohr put it beautifully:

> Jesus praises the weeping class, those who can enter into solidarity with the pain of the world and not try to extract themselves from it. That is why Jesus says the rich man can't see the Kingdom. The rich one spends life trying to make tears unnecessary and, ultimately, impossible. . . . The weeping mode allows one to carry the dark side, to bear the pain of the world

without looking for perpetrators or victims, but instead recognizing the tragic reality that both sides are caught up in. Tears from God are always *for everybody*.[5]

Luke rather impolitely adds a "Woe" to Matthew's "Blessed." "Woe to you that laugh now, for you shall mourn and weep." The Greek word for "laugh," *gelao*, connotes a chuckling that is "ironic or flippant, even haughty or foolish."[6] Christianity is not a sour-faced recipe for dullness; but we are called away from mindless frivolity. In fact, our laughter, our joy, our delight in life emerges from having taken God and each other with utmost seriousness, instead of flippantly partying our way through life.

"They Shall Be Comforted"

What miraculous antidote, what divine reply does Jesus offer to those who mourn? "They shall be comforted." We long for comfort. We know something of comfort we have given or received. We can imagine what comfort might be like. At the risk of leapfrogging prematurely into some theology Jesus didn't address in Matthew 5, we may notice that the Greek verb *paraklēthēsontai* is derived from the same root as the Comforter (*paraklētos,* "the one called to be alongside us"), which Jesus promises to the disciples on the night before his crucifixion (John 16:7). He knew that they would mourn his death, that even after the resurrection they would live with a nagging sense of his absence, that they would be sensitized to the sin, pain, and suffering of the world. So he promised he would send a Comforter.

Just who is this Comforter? The Holy Spirit. Not that Jesus is promising the Holy Spirit in the Sermon on the Mount! But how tantalizing for us, the readers, who know the full story! Those who mourn will be comforted, and at the end of the day our comfort is the Holy Spirit—but what exactly does the Spirit deliver? Saint Augustine's answer moves me: the gift of the Holy Spirit is nothing other than the Holy Spirit. God loves, and gives us not this or that, but something of immeasurably wonderful value: the Spirit's own self. The Psalmist, praying in agony, with nothing left to hang on to, prays to God in a way that no doubt moves the Holy Spirit to smile:

Whom have I in heaven but thee?
    And there is nothing upon earth that I desire besides thee.
My flesh and my heart may fail,
    but God is the strength of my heart and my portion for ever.
For lo, those who are far from thee shall perish;
. . . .
But for me it is good to be near God;
    I have made the Lord GOD my refuge.

(Ps. 73:25–28)

In a way, even in the Sermon on the Mount, the comfort Jesus offers is himself, as he invites those who mourn to follow him, to be near him.

The Spirit's comfort is like no other. My spouse may listen, care deeply, and embrace me. My friend may stay the night. My pastor may read a Psalm and say a prayer. Church folks may name me in a prayer chain or deliver a casserole. But the Spirit, who rests mightily upon my spouse, friend, and pastor, can go where no one else, not even the surest, most tender spouse or friend, can go. The Spirit delves into unseen depths of my soul, and knows me better than I know myself, feeling my suffering before I am even aware of it. And the Spirit brings a comfort more powerful, more gentle, than any combination of hugs, words, or casseroles. The Spirit is God, the Spirit is love, and the Spirit comforts me not with any thing, but with the Spirit.

Watch Out for Mourners!

We do not always warm up to extended mourning, because it feels weak, wimpish, ineffective. Don't be a crybaby! Do something! But mourning need not be the antithesis of effective action. Maybe it is the one who mourns who can really do something. Clarence Jordan, arguing that "those who mourn" are those who grieve over injustice in God's world, urges us to be "real mourners." There are fake mourners out there who say,

> "Sure, the world's in a mess, and I guess maybe I'm a bit guilty like everybody else, but what can I do about it?" What they're really saying is that they are not concerned enough about themselves or the world to look for anything to do.[7]

Mourning elicits action, courageous engagement. Having stood face-to-face with the KKK himself, and having watched friends heroically stand up for their faith and battle injustice, Jordan warned:

> You'd better watch out when a fellow gets that certain gleam in his eye and a certain set to his jaw. He's getting ready to "mourn." And he'll be awfully hard to stop, because he will be receiving tremendous strength and power and encouragement from seeing his dreams become deeds.[8]

As we will see in our next Beatitude, we may need to watch out for the "meek," who are also awfully hard to stop.

Questions for Discussion

1. Have you ever felt "blessed" in the midst of your mourning? When?
2. Have you ever felt the comfort of the Holy Spirit in the midst of your mourning? How?
3. Do you and your friends "mourn" over the injustices in God's world? In what ways?

The Meek

Blessed are the meek, for they shall inherit the earth.
—Matthew 5:5

*I*f we begin to explore the Greek word translated "meek," we may find ourselves hoping it *really* means something besides "meek," for we cannot fathom that the "meek" could be blessed. We pity the meek, we probably avoid the meek, we may poke fun at the meek behind their backs. In the Roman Empire, and in modern times, critics have mocked Christianity as a religion for weaklings.[1] Put the word "meek" on your résumé, and you'll never get a job. Maybe Jesus didn't mean what we think of as "meek."

But the Greek word, *praüs*, really does mean mild, gentle, unassuming, perhaps a bit obsequious, unable to take much initiative. An animal whose wildness has been tamed, discipline having rendered him gentle, would be called *praüs*. The meek person shyly hangs back when others are stepping forward. The meek are passive.

The meek in Jesus' crowd may not have chosen meekness; meekness is frequently forced upon you by circumstance. In Matthew 5, the meek are those treated by the world as nobodies.[2] Think of the mentality of a slave woman on a Southern plantation, or the posture of the beggar on a street in Europe, or the stare from a disease-ravaged child in Africa. To those who have no power, who have nowhere to turn and no one in their corner, Jesus says, "Blessed are the meek."

As we overhear Jesus' kind words to those who are literally meek, we should rightly assume that a spiritual attitude of meekness is implied as well. The cultivation of a holy meekness in our souls is the most daunting, uphill (or, better, we should say "downhill"!) struggle. The meek are humble, and although life in the world can be humbling, no one out there celebrates humility. When Paul wrote, "Do not be conformed to this world, but be transformed by the renewal of your mind," he targeted one type of conformity to avoid: "I bid every one . . . not to think of himself more highly than he ought to think, but to think with sober judgment" (Rom. 12:2–3). To enter into meekness, I imagine myself magically changed into the body of a wild animal that has been domesticated, or as a shy person lingering behind a pillar; I sing an old slave spiritual, or get down on my hands and knees with my hands outstretched. I think "meek," and begin to gravitate toward meekness.

The Good Hidden in Meekness

I begin to intuit the virtues of meekness. Humility is the ground of all goodness, and if I am humble, I can get out of the way so others might catch a passing glimpse of the God I love. Consider Thomas Merton's image: "The humble man receives praise the way a clean window takes the light of the sun. The truer and more intense the light is, the less you see of the glass."[3] The meek are able to be kind—and perhaps we may learn to honor and even crave meekness if this is so. For deep inside we all crave to be treated kindly, and know we have missed golden opportunities to show kindness. "When death, the great Reconciler, has come, it is never our tenderness that we repent of, but our severity" (George Eliot).[4]

The meek are able to receive direction. Jesus' reference point, the hinge upon which divine meekness swivels, is not the powers of the world: the "meek" are not those who cave in to every whim of society, who let themselves be trampled by the boss, who endure cruel abuse at the hands of a dominating spouse. They "do not allow themselves to be dragged along by the tides of political power or to be led by the smell of money. Such rudderless persons have cut themselves off from . . . God's voice in their heart" (Jim Forest).[5] Jesus is interested in meekness toward God, being directable by God. A directable meekness, a leadable weakness, is not a handicap, but the opening for God to use us. Remember Paul's words? "The Spirit helps us in our weakness; for we do not know how to pray as we ought, but that very Spirit intercedes for us with sighs too deep for words" (Rom. 8:26, mg.).

You do not need to be aggressive to make a relationship with God happen. In fact, you cannot make it happen. To know God, to live as close as possible to Jesus, to be fundamentally altered by the Spirit as your rudder, you must have what John Calvin called a "teachable spirit" (docilitas in Latin, whose cognate you may recognize: "docile").[6] Living the Christian life: this is not something I do. Jesus said, Blessed are the meek, the humble, the happily docile, the nobly weak. Jesus did not say, Blessed are the smart, the theologically agile, the spiritual giants.

Small Is Beautiful

Perhaps a look at some fictional non-giants may be instructive. J. R. R. Tolkien's duly famous and fabulously successful books, The Hobbit and the Lord of the Rings trilogy (and films), narrate the exploits of hobbits, diminutive characters in this epic fantasy who have no epic ambitions at all. They are childlike in stature, content to stick to the Shire; they feel no urges to own much or travel anywhere. So why do we adore and cheer for these hobbits? And why is their unlikely triumph over evil so exciting? Is it more than merely pulling for the underdog? Is it an unwitting recognition of what is wrong with the way we gawk after what is impressive? Ralph Wood suggests that "Tolkien makes them diminutive creatures in order to challenge our obsession with largeness. For the hobbits, bigger does not mean better, and small can indeed be beautiful."[7]

The hobbits live, not in a towering fortress, but in small earthen huts. Hobbits are "shy of the Big People."[8] They are not consumers; they give presents to others on their own birthdays; they are unfailingly supportive in friendship—as they must be, precisely because they are small! Lacking in acquisitiveness and lust for power, they are the ideal protagonists to destroy the ring of power, for they alone don't want power, which corrupts those big people who pant for it in their desire to be even bigger. The story then turns on these unlikely heroes:

> The world being full after all of strange creatures beyond count, these little people seemed of very little importance. But in the days of Bilbo, and of Frodo his heir, they suddenly became, by no wish of their own, both important and renowned, and troubled the counsels of the Wise and the Great.[9]

Boasting neither war machines nor titanic powers, the hobbits find themselves on a quest, and all of history turns on their reaching the final destination. Elrond, the elvish king, spoke in admiration of them: "Such is oft the course of deeds that move the wheels of the world: small hands do them because they must, while the eyes of the great are elsewhere."[10]

Tolkien is mirroring the curious way of God in the Scriptures, isn't he? Didn't Moses chuckle over God's choice of the Israelites? "It was not because you were more in number than any other people that the LORD set his love upon you and chose you, for you were the fewest of all peoples" (Deut. 7:7). Moses himself was "very meek, more than all men that were on the face of the earth" (Num. 12:3); little wonder Moses could hear God speaking so clearly and often! Didn't God tell Gideon thirty-two thousand warriors were *too many* for God to use to defeat the Midianites, and the battle was not waged until a mere three hundred were left (Judg. 7)? Didn't Samuel pass over the mighty older sons of Jesse before anointing little David, who in turn toppled the giant Goliath (1 Sam. 16–17)? Didn't God call nations on the carpet with a mere boy named Jeremiah? The meek do not mind being weak, for their strength is entirely in God; as Martin Luther put it, "Faith is the humility that turns its back on its own reason and strength."[11]

The Cloak of Folly

Wasn't the Virgin Mary the epitome of meekness? Her simple, calm life having been invaded by an unsolicited angelic message, disrupting her plans, requiring an openness to the unfathomable, she replied, "Let it be to me according to your word" (Luke 1:38). Didn't Paul say, "the foolishness of God is wiser than men, and the weakness of God is stronger than men. For consider your call, brethren; not many of you were wise according to worldly standards, not many were powerful, not many were of noble birth; but God chose what is foolish in the world to shame the wise, God chose what is weak in the world to shame the strong, God chose what is low and despised in the world . . . to bring to nothing things that are, so that no human being might boast" (1 Cor. 1:25–29)? If this be folly, then, as Gandalf, the grey wizard and friend of the hobbits, said, "Let folly be our cloak."[12]

Blessed are the meek, who wear folly as their cloak! Paul's gravest concern was our tendency to "boast." The meek are (as we have seen) "humble." Jim Forest directs our attention to the story of Abba Macarius, a fourth-century monk in Egypt, who met up with the devil on the road. Attacking repeatedly, yet without success, the devil asked, "What is your power, Macarius, that makes me powerless against you? All that you do, I do too. You fast, but I never eat. You keep vigil, but I never sleep. In one thing only do you beat me." Abba Macarius asked what that was. The devil said, "Your humility. Because of that I can do nothing against you."[13]

Notice that Macarius does not lift up his spiritual résumé and declare, "It is because of my humility." It is Lancelot du Lac, in *Camelot*, who boasts of his *humilité* when quizzed by Guinevere about the source of prowess—and as the story unfolds we discover that the one who is proud of his humility suffers that most tumultuous fall, for his humility was nothing but the charade of the egomaniac. Macarius is clueless: his utter humility is something he has never noticed, like the back of his own head, as he is attentive to God and entirely unfocused on his own self.

Inherit the Earth

So what is the destiny of Macarius, Mary, David, the hobbits, and the rest of the meek? "They will inherit the earth." Jesus promises a jolting reversal of the haves and the have-nots—and this future grabs our attention so we might pay heed to St. Augustine's warning: "You who wish to possess the earth now, take care. If you are meek, you will possess it; if ruthless, the earth will possess you."[14] Seizing our piece of the pie, striving to possess a sizable chunk of earth now, is to walk a path of deception. The possess*ive* find it all but impossible to avoid being possess*ed*; our possessions possess us, and the pursuit of a grand inheritance disinherits us. To be near Jesus, we stick as nearly as possible with the meek.

Out of the pit, God will catapult the meek to the heights. Beggars will be ridiculously rich. Of course, this does not mean that if you pass the divine meekness test, God will reward you with millions so you can live on a heavenly island someplace. These heirs who inherit are in a family that forever remains meek. These heirs are co-inheritors of the kingdom of heaven, and instead of licking their chops and saying, "Finally I've got what's coming to me," they leave the kingdom in the hands of the Lord of the kingdom, and for the benefit of others. For the lone good the meek have always pursued will then be theirs: proximity to Jesus.

Even now, the meek wield a curious kind of transforming power. When Peter and the apostles were arrested, they stood before steely authorities and announced meekly, "We must obey God rather than men" (Acts 5:29). Consider the power of nonviolent resisters in Gandhi's India, or in America during the civil rights era: black men dressed in suits, singing hymns, being hosed down and bitten by dogs in Bull Connor's Birmingham; Martin Luther King Jr. repeatedly slapped in the face by an angry Klansman. Back when he was still a teenager, John Lewis (who, years later, was elected to Congress) was arrested for his role in a nonviolent demonstration. He had grown up terrified of prison, and was no less fearful that Saturday morning. But,

> as they took him from the downtown store and fingerprinted him, the fear fell from him, and he felt as if a great burden had been lifted from his shoulders. He felt his own strength growing. As the cops arrested his group he had looked at the faces of his friends and had seen the same thing he felt himself. He did not, as he had sometimes feared in the past few months, feel small and vulnerable. He felt empowered, part of something much larger than himself. . . . Years later he could point out the photos of the very young John Lewis coming out of jail on that day, and note that there it was in his face, the confidence, the dignity. *I had never had that much dignity before*, he said years later. *It was exhilarating.*[15]

Blessed are the meek. Powerful are the meek! A holy meekness can change the face of society, and the earth to be inherited will never be the same.

As a footnote, we have neglected thus far to mention that the Greek word translated meek in Matthew 5:5 is not just one *praüs* ("meek" in the singular), but is actually *praeîs* ("meek" in the plural). "The meek" isn't the single, lonely meek individual. Generally, anyone with meekness is isolated, marginalized, and left alone. But Jesus uses the plural, suggesting there is a community, some sense of belonging, among the meek.

When Jesus pledges the earth itself to the meek, he has no plans to divvy it up so each individual meek person can have a little slice of the pie. A new family is being birthed, and the meek inherit the earth together as one family or not at all. But we would expect this of the meek, for they do not advance their own private agendas, they are not competitive, they aren't trying to get ahead. The world competes, compares, beats, gets beaten, distinguishes, grabs, and measures. But the meek are near enough to Jesus that they never compare or make distinctions that divide, for Jesus never grades or squashes one person down on top of somebody else. Blessed are the meek, plural, all of them in a new family of mutual deference and humble kindness.

Questions for Discussion

1. In what ways has your perception of "meekness" changed by reading this chapter?
2. What are some implications of Luther's saying that "Faith is the humility that turns its back on its own reason and strength"?
3. What are some examples you've experienced of the power of those who are "meek"?

Hunger and Thirst

Blessed are those who hunger and thirst for righteousness.
—Matthew 5:6

We should be experts at satisfaction, as no people in the history of this planet have ever enjoyed so much affluence, such a broad range of choice, such unbridled freedom—and yet Mick Jagger's rock lyric still touches a nerve: "I can't get no satisfaction . . . I try, and I try, and I try, and I try." We try; we may actually be connoisseurs in the satisfaction of hunger and thirst, with professionals poised to satisfy—the maître d', the bartender, the grocer—who require no more than a credit card. We have even turned to the spiritual, scooping up the latest books, shopping for a preacher or praise band, surfing channels for somebody with a miracle up his sleeve. So why is hollowness so rampant? And depression such an epidemic? Why is there a malaise, a sense that something is missing? Why do we ricochet from one relationship to another, one restaurant to another, one diversion to another, and still happiness, contentment, peace seem just out of reach?

We set ourselves up, or at least somebody did. We are reared to expect a broad satisfaction, physically and emotionally—and yet on Madison Avenue, clever advertising professionals are staying up late tonight hatching novel plans to create a sense of dissatisfaction in you! Combine that with material advances in technology, with every tick upward in the stock market with each passing generation, and our unreasonable expectations that not just some but most of our desires will be satisfied gain steam. This is the great pledge of the booming capitalist economy in the land of freedom. We are free! And we exercise our freedom to choose, expecting that our choices will satisfy and that the more choices we have, the higher the likelihood that we will in fact be even more satisfied.

Too Many Choices

Quite apart from the message of Jesus, studies are exposing the fallacy of this mentality. Barry Schwartz of Swarthmore College has studied our consuming scientifically—and personally, as a shopper himself. Echoing exactly what happened to me a couple of years ago, Schwartz tells of going to the mall to replace his worn-out 32 × 28 blue jeans. The salesperson surprised him with a wide array of choices: slim fit? easy fit? relaxed? stonewashed? acid-washed? distressed? button-fly? zipper-fly?

> I was stunned. A moment or two later I sputtered out something like, "I just want regular jeans. You know, the kind that used to be the only kind." It turned out she didn't know. . . . The trouble was that with all these options available to me now, I was no longer sure that "regular" jeans were what I wanted.

So Schwartz began a consultation with the salesperson, learning about the various fits, studying a diagram, trying all of them on (and taking a considerable amount of time to do so) before selecting.

> Whereas very little was riding on my decision, I was now convinced that one of these options had to be right for me, and I was determined to figure it out. But I couldn't. Finally I chose the easy fit, because "relaxed fit" implied I was getting soft in the middle and needed to cover it up. . . . By creating all these options, the store undoubtedly had done a favor for customers with varied tastes and body types. However, by vastly expanding the range of choices, they also created a new problem that needed to be solved. Now it was a complex decision in which I was forced to invest time, energy, and no small amount of self-doubt, anxiety, and dread.[1]

Studies corroborate his suspicion: endlessly expanded choice does not bring the perfect life, but merely teases and disappoints, leading to anxiety and depression. People are shopping more (far more often than they go to places of worship!), but enjoying it less. Among teenage girls, 93 percent of those surveyed named "shopping" as their favorite activity—but teenagers are suffering epidemic levels of boredom and depression. When a given choice may well be "good enough," we press on for the "best possible" choice—and not merely when selecting among 137 kinds of pasta sauces on the grocery shelf, or among 58 types of cell phones on the Internet, or what to watch among two hundred-plus cable channels, or choosing from among hundreds of jackets in a catalog (with the added anxiety-inducing issue of finding the best price), but also when choosing a cardiologist or an oncologist, or choosing a spouse.

The illusion is that, given so many good choices, we can arrange just the right life. But then we get tangled in the inevitabilities of real life, and we begin to look back with a squadron of "if only's": if only I had bought the Honda instead, if only I had picked AOL, if only I hadn't asked Sherri to marry me, if only I had taken medical treatment B instead of medical treatment A when the doctor asked what I wanted to do. Modern Americans "enjoy" more choice, freedom, and autonomy—so why do we suffer so psychologically?

Don't we see how being adept at consuming robs us of any possibility of gratitude? If I am in control, making all the selections, satisfying my whims, how could I ever humbly imagine myself to be a receiver, terribly lucky to have anything at all? Schwartz's studies demonstrate that the few people who feel and express gratitude are healthier and more energetic!

Don't we see how unbridled freedom of choice destroys relationships? To be a friend, to be married, to join a church: all these imply a decrease in choice and autonomy. I take on responsibilities, I limit my choices, I refuse to dabble in "what-ifs." Don't we see how, if we throw ourselves with abandon into the freedom-of-choice mind-set, we will never discover what God is calling us to do, who God made us to be? Schwartz, lamenting the overload of the thousands of little choices we must make that previous generations never had to deal with, notices that we are under unwitting pressure "to create an identity rather than to accept a given identity."[2]

Little wonder that the church (if we don't sell out and pervert our message by feeding into the consumer mentality) faces massive obstacles when we try to get our message out: we declare that you have a given identity, that your freedom of choice is not much more than a chaotic exercise in sinfulness, that if we are to do anything with the hungering and thirsting we all experience, it should be to go and find some righteousness, which alone can satisfy. Maggie Ross is right: "We feel empty, but feeling has little to do with being empty."[3] Don't we feel empty because we are full of the wrong stuff?

The Hunger of Jesus' Crowd

The time gap between our day and that of Jesus is nowhere more unfathomably wide. Those who were in earshot of Jesus had no choices whatsoever. Hunger and thirst were not spiritual metaphors, but the reality of the daily grind. Trying to eke out enough to eat, battling the elements (from rocks in the soil to brigands, insects, and blight), enduring exhaustion and illness (for which the doctors of antiquity probably did more harm than good), only to feel the harsh fist of the tax collector seizing half of what wasn't nearly enough to begin with, Jesus' listeners were quite literally hungry and thirsty.

We can therefore understand the heady appeal of messianic expectation. Everyone who listened to Jesus believed that, when the Messiah comes, our crops will grow, our storehouses will be full, the wine will flow plentifully. When God's deliverance comes, this voice will be heard:

> "Ho, every one who thirsts,
>   come to the waters;
> and he who has no money,
>   come, buy and eat!
> Come, buy wine and milk
>   without money and without price."
> (Isa. 55:1)

What will the messianic kingdom look like?

> On this mountain the LORD of hosts will make for all peoples a feast of fat things, a feast of wine on the lees, of fat things full

of marrow. . . . It will be said on that day, "Lo, this is our God; we have waited for him, that he might save us. . . . Let us be glad and rejoice in his salvation." (Isa. 25:6, 9)

The righteous indeed were hungry for that day when God will vindicate the elect, when God's will would be embodied on earth.

Jesus spoke to people who had a developed sense of this word "righteousness." The Old Testament, throughout the Law and the Prophets, lifted up "righteousness" as the goal of human existence. "Righteousness" carries undertones of the dream that God will vindicate his people and crush their evil oppressors. But more pointedly, "righteousness" is a life lived in conformity to God's will, adhering to God's laws, a life of prayerful holiness. The "righteous" let their hearts and heads be dominated by God's vision for life down here; and this "righteousness" is never merely spiritual, but is expressed in specific, concrete acts.

The word connotes being straight, strong, steadfast. Mark Helprin wrote of a young boy, Levi, who learned much from his grandfather, "that soft lesson that became the steel of his life."[4] Blessed are the poor in spirit, those who weep, the meek, those who hunger and thirst for righteousness; blessed is that softness, that tenderness, which is the firm steel of the soul.

By the time Matthew wrote down his Gospel, this word "righteousness" (*dikaiosune*) had zoomed to the top of Christianity's theological vocabulary list. In Paul's profound understanding of the effects of Jesus' life and death, "righteousness" is transformed from something we are supposed to *do* to something that God *gives*. Righteousness is a gift from God, achieved by Jesus. Righteousness for Paul is really a wrong relationship with God that has been set right—not by us, but by God.

But is this really so different? Isn't right behavior, a holy adherence to God's law, nothing more than the tangible expression of a relationship with God? Certainly in the Beatitudes, Jesus blesses those who hunger and thirst for a righteousness that is first and foremost a relationship with Jesus the teacher, Jesus the pioneer, Jesus the one headed to crucifixion and resurrection. The changed life grows out of that, or doesn't happen at all. The hunger and thirst are for Jesus himself.

Making a Connection

Now once again we are on familiar ground: we know hunger and thirst for a relationship. In Pat Conroy's novel *The Lords of Discipline*, young Will McLean laments his lack of a romantic life with words that may reflect our anxiety about God:

> I once read in a book that traced the natural history of blue whales that the great creatures often had to travel thousands of miles through the dark waters of the Pacific to find a mate. They conducted their search with the fever and furious attention of beasts aware of the imminence of extinction. As whaling fleets depleted their numbers, scientists conjectured that there were whales who would exhaust themselves in fruitless wandering and never connect with any mate at all. When I read about those solitary leviathans, I feared I had stumbled on an allegory of my own life, that I would spend my life unable to make a connection, unable to find someone attracted by the beauty and urgency of my song.[5]

We crave intimacy, a deep relationship—with anybody, although God would be a particularly appealing partner. We understand the Psalmist who saw a deer sniffing the air, peering into a dry riverbed, searching for water, and perceived in this beautiful creature an image of his own quest for God:

> As a hart longs for flowing streams,
> so longs my soul for thee, O God.
> (Ps. 42:1)

But as we contemplate this quest, as we weigh what it means nowadays to have "seeker" services, as we measure the meaning of spirituality in our culture and our lives, we may pause over an issue Jesus perhaps anticipated.

Yearning, not Possession

Notice that Jesus did not say, "Blessed are those who *are* righteous," but, "Blessed are those who *hunger and thirst for* righteousness." If you think you possess it, you become self-righteous. God fashioned the hollowness inside us, not as an evil to be cured, but as the most marvelous gift. The popular hymn "Fill My Cup, Lord" gets it wrong: "Feed me 'til I want no more." Jesus wants us to keep wanting. The great theologians and spiritual heroes of history have never claimed that they were fully fed, satiated, the way we slide back into our easy chair after a plenteous Thanksgiving feast. We hunger and thirst for righteousness. The beauty is in the hungering, in the yearning. The nagging hankering we feel inside is God's voice, calling us home, keeping us a bit "restless until we find rest in God" (to recall Augustine's phrase).

Gregory of Nyssa, back in the fourth century in Cappadocia, wrote eloquently of the way God gives us just a tantalizing taste of God's presence, a hazy glimpse of God's utter beauty, only to draw us forward again as if we had never tasted that beauty, as if we were still straining to see it for the first time. Gregory thought of Moses' intimacy with God: "Moses' desire is filled by the very fact that it remains unfulfilled. . . . And this is the real meaning of seeing God: never to have this desire satisfied."[6] For Gregory, true satisfaction "consists in constantly going on in the quest and never ceasing in ascent, seeing that every fulfillment . . . continually generates a further desire." This discovery, "far from making the soul despair, is actually an experience of God's fuller presence. It becomes a yearning which fills the soul more fully than any actual possession."[7]

So Jesus is not in a rush to slake our thirst, to banish our hunger. We relate to Jesus as a deer longing for flowing streams, as a beggar seeking bread, as a lover singing a lyric to the beloved long before they have consummated their passion. The dissatisfaction we feel is what draws us toward righteousness. We who find ourselves on the ladder of the Beatitudes need the poverty, mourning, and meekness that drive our hunger for God, not settling prematurely for a sense of fullness, not demanding that God fill my cup until I want no more. I want to want God. Augustine was right:

If we acknowledge ourselves as thirsting, we shall acknowledge ourselves as drinking also. For he that thirsteth in this world, in the world to come shall be satisfied, according to the Lord's saying, *Blessed are they that hunger and thirst for righteousness, for the same shall be satisfied.* Therefore in this world we ought not to love fullness.[8]

So those who hunger and thirst may well embrace a habit that only superficially runs contrary to the goal of the hungry: fasting. When we fast, we actually heighten our hunger, not as spiritual vanity, but to feel more intensely our hunger for God, and to feel that hunger in at least a temporary solidarity with the physically hungry in God's world.

Only righteousness, only a relationship with the living Lord, can satisfy—but even that satisfaction leaves us hungry for more. The best, most scintillating taste of that righteousness is offered to us at the Lord's Table. We come forward to the altar, hungry beyond description for the presence of the Lord, for meaning and purpose, for goodness and life. The priest hands us just a fragment of bread. We take just a tiny sip of wine. Just enough to make you want more. And more. Blessed are those who hunger and thirst for righteousness, for they shall be filled.

In that hunger, we can then endure the loss of everything else. A close, intimate relationship is like that: it can enjoy good things but bear their loss, can be content with whatever comes, can withstand every disaster. Thomas Merton, reflecting on the inevitable losses we suffer, wrote (in a letter to Dorothy Day) that persevering in our relationship with God isn't

a matter of getting a bulldog grip on faith and not letting the devil pry us loose from it. No, it is a matter of letting go rather than keeping hold. I am coming to think God . . . loves and helps best those who are so beat and have so much nothing when they come to die that it is almost as if they had persevered in nothing but had gradually lost everything, piece by piece, until there was nothing left but God. . . . It is a question of his hanging on to us, by the hair of the head, that is from on top and beyond, where we cannot see or reach. What man can see the top of his own head?[9]

This being hung onto where we cannot reach: we call this mercy.

Questions for Discussion

1. What are some examples of when having more "choices" does not "satisfy" us?
2. What are you "hungering and thirsting" for in your life?
3. In what ways are you "hungering and thirsting for righteousness"?

Merciful

Blessed are the merciful, for they shall obtain mercy.
—Matthew 5:7

*T*his fifth Beatitude is unique: it is reflexive. While the poor in spirit receive the kingdom, or the meek inherit the earth, those who show mercy receive exactly what they just showed: mercy. The reward of mercy is . . . mercy. Was Jesus not quick enough on his feet to think of a different word? Or is a secret unveiled? Does Jesus, perhaps with a wink, commend the merciful, knowing all too well that the hidden key that unlocks the treasure of being merciful is our receiving mercy?

Mercy has evaporated from the landscape of our culture, leaving us dry, crusty, hardened. We are a permissive people, but then we show no mercy. Could it be that we will have to remember how to be merciful before we can get our house in order and ratchet up our moral zeal as a people? Mercy requires a high standard, doesn't it? Our inability to show mercy wars against our ability to receive mercy (or to be genuinely good, not just a fake)—which wars against our ability to be merciful . . . and so the cold, steely circle is forged.

Henri Nouwen wrote a lovely devotional reflection on Rembrandt's painting of *The Return of the Prodigal Son*, which provoked him to wonder how much mercy he had missed in his busy, controlled life: "Had I really ever dared to step into the center, kneel down, and let myself be held by a forgiving God?" instead of "choosing over and over again the position of the outsider looking in."[1] We are interested in Christ, and perhaps we have heard his voice, asking us to cry for the mercy he tenderly provides; so why do we linger out on the periphery?

Other Loud Voices

Nouwen helps us to see that "there are many other voices, voices that are loud, full of promises and very seductive. These voices say, 'Go out and prove that you are worth something.'" Do you know these voices as I do? They cut deep inside into those vulnerable recesses where we doubt our worth, where we know we can never achieve enough; they wrap "what I do" around "who I am" and cruelly lie to us. "They suggest that I am not going to be loved without my having earned it. They want me to prove to myself and others that I am worth being loved. They deny loudly that love is a totally free gift."[2] And so these ruminations rumble through my soul all day long, largely undetected but never very far beneath the surface. And so we live our lives within earshot of Jesus, but never up close, foolishly twisting away from the tender arms of the One who said, "Blessed are the merciful, for they shall receive mercy."

How distant is "mercy" from all the ad campaigns with which we are peppered? They curiously pander to me, saying, "You deserve only the best mattress," "You deserve a new car," "You deserve a week in the Bahamas." These billboards do not know me, but they drive me away from mercy, which has nothing to do with deserving. We are so practiced at self-justification, at rationalizing and explaining. We feel entitled. I'm owed a good life, and if I don't get it, I get busy blaming somebody. And so, mercy is a stranger. Even when we speak of heaven, "deserving" vaunts itself: Mr. Jones, an elderly do-gooder at the church dies; and what do people say? "If anybody gets into heaven, it will be Mr. Jones. Look at all he did!" And we never find ourselves inside the circle, kneeling, embraced by the loving arms of the Father—we stay outside, spectating, looking in, never knowing mercy.

What is mercy? Think back over your life. Mercy is not something we define so much as something for which we cry out in desperation. A kid is about to pound the daylights out of me on the playground, and what am I required to say out loud? "Mercy." A terrible, horrible mistake has been made, smashing a well-arranged life, and your regret is so intense no strategy can extricate you from the mess, and the only cry left to make is "Mercy." You gaze at the crucifix, and you keep looking, letting it nestle jarringly down into the marrow of your self, and finally you get it, and the only plea you know you must make, yet that you can make, is, "Mercy."

Deep inside, don't you crave mercy? To be loved despite your craziness, to be handled tenderly? And don't we need to be tender, merciful, forgiving to others? We are such hard, tough, cool, smooth, crusty people—but how sad, how tragic. Blessed are the merciful, for they shall receive mercy. We are not very open to mercy, and so we are not so merciful, and so we receive no mercy. Jesus anticipated that this Beatitude would have to be reflexive—just as he did when he taught the disciples to pray, "Forgive us our debts, as we forgive our debtors" (or "Forgive us our trespasses as we forgive those who trespass against us"). Forgive as we forgive; the merciful shall receive mercy.[3]

Dignity and Mercy

How hard is it to be merciful? Mercy is not doing nothing. The Greek word *eleos* suggests the connotation of pouring out, the way we might pour out a flask of oil. Mercy is a pouring out. Mercy is when I unscrew the lid on what is precious to me and pour it out on you. I may not think I have all that much to pour out, but the merciful pour anyway, thinking only of the wounded one who needs the healing balm of mercy. Noting how beleaguered Jesus' listeners were, Bonhoeffer adds,

> As if their own needs and their own distress were not enough, they take upon themselves the distress and humiliation and sin of others. They have an irresistible love for the downtrodden, the sick, the wretched, the wronged, the outcast, and all who are tortured with anxiety. No distress is too great, no sin too appalling for their pity. If any man falls into disgrace, the merciful will sacrifice their own honour to shield him, and take his shame upon themselves. In order that they may be merciful, they cast away the most priceless treasure of human life, their personal dignity and honour. For the only honour and dignity they know is their Lord's own mercy, to which alone they owe their very lives.[4]

This wisdom bears repetition, and much reflection. The merciful are far less interested in their own honor than in mercy; their only honor is mercy. The merciful do not get tangled in a thicket of who deserves what, or calculations of whether their mercy will be productive or not. The merciful are merciful because they have received mercy from the same Jesus who said, "Blessed are the merciful, for they shall obtain mercy." Bonhoeffer saw the heart of this thought: "Only he who lives by the forgiveness of his sin in Jesus Christ will rightly think little of himself. He will know that his own wisdom reached the end of its tether when Jesus forgave him."[5]

Mercy eludes those who are shocked and mortified by sin or suffering. The merciful get so absorbed in God's mercy that they see sin and suffering differently. The merciful are never offended by anything, for they have lost interest in sin, so fascinated are they by God's mercy. The Beatitudes truly are a ladder. For it is only the poor in spirit who can be merciful. Those who mourn know more keenly than anyone else how to be merciful. The meek have no reason not to be merciful. Those who hunger and thirst for righteousness understand that mercy is their food and drink.

"Merciful" is not just an inner attitude, although it *is* an inner attitude. "Merciful" is something you do. You plan to get busy being merciful, but then you are prepared at a moment's notice to let the schedule be shredded, for, like that Good Samaritan, you see somebody beaten up by the side of the road, and instead of guessing why he's in the pickle he's in, instead of being so ultraresponsible as to be punctual for your next meeting, you are merciful. Otherwise we live merely in earshot of Jesus, and never get close to the one who said, "Blessed are the merciful," the one who was and is Mercy itself.

How revolutionary! How liberating! Mercy frees me from self-centeredness. Pouring myself out of my own ego trap is the way to joy. Wendy Farley put it pointedly: "Liberation from the tedious weight of one's own miserable little ego is not necessarily self-sacrificing but can be profoundly fulfilling."[6] Mercy frees me from the need to "fix" whatever is wrong. Mercy is able quite simply to love, to be compassionate, whether the hurt is curable or not, whether the wrong can be righted or not. Mercy can just stay with the one in need of mercy.

And in mercy I show respect, I shed dignity on the one whose self-respect and sense of dignity have been shredded. Mercy does not spout forth all the answers. Job's friends were not very merciful friends, for they pontificated theologically about the presumed causes of his suffering, when really he needed friends to weep and sit in the dirt with him. Mercy has no need to justify or explain. Mercy never trivializes suffering with trite explanations of "why." Mercy listens, gets inside the other's skin, letting the tears soak into your own shoulder. For as we show mercy, and receive mercy, our hearts are purged and we are awestruck to glimpse some purity inside.

Questions for Discussion

1. Why do you think it is so difficult for people to "show mercy"?
2. In what incidents of your life have you shown mercy? been granted mercy?
3. In what ways does God show mercy to us?

10

Pure in Heart

Blessed are the pure in heart.

—Matthew 5:8

*F*or Jesus, as for all people in Bible times, the "heart" was not a pulsating organ inside your chest to be strengthened by exercise and a good diet or cured by the cardiologist's tool kit. The heart is your truest self. The heart is the part of you that feels, delights, grieves, desires. The heart is the "imagination," the place inside where we conceive, where we make connections, where we dream. The heart is the place where you exercise your freedom, where you decide, the mechanism that chooses what to do this evening, whom you will marry, whether to lie or not, how to respond to a crisis. The heart is the sphere where we meet God, or avoid meeting God.

So what is a "pure heart"? The Greek word *katharoi* implies being clean, unpolluted, with a hint that what is pure was not always pure, but has been purified, cleansed, washed out, and hung up to dry. A "catharsis" (derived from *katharoi*) is an emotional resolution (as when a story reaches its climax and the reader has a rush of realization); the *Oxford English Dictionary* somewhat less elegantly defines "catharsis" as "a purgation, especially the evacuation of the bowels." The pure heart would be a heart that has been emptied of what is unclean, purged of what no longer belongs.

"Blessed are the pure in heart." It may be helpful to think of purity in two ways. There is a purity that looks like simplicity, focus, single-mindedness; and there is a purity that looks like good-ness, cleanness, holiness—and the two are not unrelated. And neither is championed in our culture. Søren Kierkegaard wrote a duly famous book entitled *Purity of Heart Is to Will One Thing.* The human predica-ment is that we let ourselves get frittered away in multiple directions, trying to be and do everything, when we were made for just one thing, for *the one* thing that finally matters: God. If purity of heart is "to will one thing," then focus is everything. The pure, like a racehorse, need "blinders" to block out their peripheral vision, so they keep their eyes on the one goal, straight ahead, the finish line.

"To Will One Thing"

Jesus' visit to Mary and Martha portrays a pure heart—and one heart that is not. Martha upbraids Mary for not helping her with the meal preparations. But Jesus praises Mary and exposes Martha's distracted complexity: "Martha, Martha, you are anxious and troubled about many things; one thing is needful" (Luke 10:41–42). The pure in heart do not let themselves be carved up into a thousand pieces; they are singular in mind, they stay in one place, riveted on one thing.

Our diffuse, scattered lives do come into focus on occasion, whether we seek purity of heart or not. The phone rings in the middle of the night, or the doctor informs you that "it is malignant," or some-one runs a red light. Suddenly your calendar, which loomed over you as a relentless taskmaster just moments before, flies out the window, and nothing else matters but the one thing. Anna Quindlen's novel *One True Thing* tells the story of a daughter who leaves her life and career to care for her mother, who is dying of cancer. Her love for her mother was "the one true thing." When asked, "Did you love your mother?" she replied,

> The easy answer is yes. But it's too easy just to say that when you're talking about your mother. It's so much more than love—it's, it's everything, isn't it? When someone asks you where you come from, the answer is your mother. When your mother's gone, you've lost your past. It's so much more than love. Even when there's no love, it's so much more than anything else in

your life. I did love my mother, but I didn't know how much until she was gone.[1]

Months passed, and then as she looked back, she had to confess that

what was important . . . was that we had so misunderstood her, this woman who had made us who we were while we barely noticed it. . . . And being so wrong about her makes me wonder now how often I am utterly wrong about myself.[2]

Purity of heart is to will one thing. To use Quindlen's words, purity of heart is about our relationship that is really more than love with the one from whom we all came. We would have our hearts purified, for we are a mess of misunderstandings about God, and therefore we are a mess of misunderstandings about ourselves. One thing is needful. Blessed are the pure in heart. The wounds we mourn in life can bring the needed healing, yielding what Marilynne Robinson called "an earned innocence."[3]

To Will the Right Thing

But if purity of heart is to will one thing, that one thing can't be just any old thing. We may will the penthouse office in the corporate tower, or we may will the glamour of being thought cool or good-looking. Our swiftest plunge away from God is when we scale the heights for what is impressive, or when we settle back for what is easy, instead of pressing for what is good. The pure in heart will the one thing that is genuinely and enduringly good. They want God, and no substitute will do.

Impurity is everywhere, seemingly wafted along in the very air we breathe. Impurity is on the television, is overheard in conversation, and has taken up unwelcome residence in my soul and yours. Part of impurity's lure is that it seems to pay. Who's getting ahead in the world? And who seems to be happy? Not the pure, not any more than the poor in spirit, the mourners, or the meek! When I ruminate darkly on such matters, I turn to my favorite Psalm, the 73rd, which begins,

"Truly God is good to the . . . pure in heart. But as for me, . . . all the day long I have been stricken." The psalmist has kept a pure heart, has done the right thing, has been faithful and good—but has been rewarded with nothing but suffering, physical pain, actual poverty. If there is a good God, how can this be? Isn't God supposed to bless?

Through the prism of tears, the Psalmist sees the fiction that the good are rewarded and the wicked are punished. Tempted to give up on God, the Psalmist "went into the sanctuary of God." He went to the temple, the holy place, and somehow by being in that place he caught some glimpse of hope. The presence of God can do things to a person, especially one who is suffering. The Psalmist is not miraculously healed. His flesh and heart are still failing. He doesn't win the lottery; he is still poor. But he affirms now, with a previously unfathomed certainty, that "God is good to the pure in heart."

For him, God is no longer the great cashier in the sky, who rings up your good deeds, and with a big "thank-you" hands you some payout. No, God is the one whose love never fails, the one who is there, who is not trivialized by human schemes of deserving. For Christians, that God has a face, and the contours of that face are the compassion and wisdom and tenderness of Jesus.

"It Is Good to Be Near God"

And God is *good*. But the *good* that God gives is no "thing." What God gives isn't this or that. God gives God's own self. I have things that belonged to my grandfather, Papa Howell: his pocket watch, his mail pouch, his Bible, some tools—and I treasure them above most earthly possessions. But I would eagerly throw them all away to have just one more hour with him, the man himself, talking, laughing, sitting under his oak tree. *For me it is good to be near God.* Legend has it that when St. Thomas Aquinas, one of the most prolific and profound theologians the church has ever known, was on his deathbed, a voice was heard from somewhere above: "Thomas, you have written well of me. What reward would you ask for yourself?" And Thomas replied, "Nothing but yourself, O Lord."[4]

God is good to the *pure in heart*. Purity of heart is no longer just doing nice things, or avoiding grimy things. In fact, no impurity of heart is more defiling than self-righteousness! Bonhoeffer wisely suggested that the pure in heart are "those whose hearts are undefiled by their own evil—and by their own virtues too."[5] What comes out of the heart? Not a mountain of good deeds, but *love*.

The pure of heart love. Jim Forest observes that not only did Jesus not say, "Blessed are the pure in mind," but that he furthermore didn't say, "Blessed are the brilliant in mind."[6] I have a cousin with Down's syndrome, and though her mind is not brilliant, her heart is brilliant, her heart is pure. She loves, more simply than the rest of us Howells with our degrees and book learning. Purity of heart is a childlike simplicity. The Beatitudes truly are a ladder: Who has a chance to be pure in heart? The poor in spirit, those who mourn, the meek, those who hunger and thirst for righteousness, the merciful—the ones who love God and love as God loves.

That's what eternal life is about: it's not that we die and then God gives us this ultimate prize. Rather, we develop a relationship of love with God now that is so strong that even death itself cannot sever it. Sorrow is always mingled with love, but that is our glory. In Rian Malan's lovely novel set in South Africa, *My Traitor's Heart*, the most compelling character is named Creina Alcock. She has suffered much. But late in life, she says this:

> Love is worth nothing until it has been tested by its own defeat. Love, even if it ends in defeat, gives you a kind of honor; without love, you have no honor at all. Love enables you to transcend defeat. Love is the only thing that leaves light inside you, instead of the total, obliterating darkness.[7]

Blessed are the pure in heart, who will one thing, who will *the one thing*, who love, with a love that can bear any defeat. Such pure lovers are not the same people they were before they found themselves in Jesus' words. Thomas Merton wrote that "purity of heart . . . means the renunciation of all deluded images of ourselves, all exaggerated estimates of our own capacities, in order to obey God's will as it comes to us in the difficult demands of life in its exacting truth. Purity of heart is then correlative to a new spiritual identity."[8]

"They Shall See God"

So what is the blessedness of the pure in heart? "They shall see God." So it must be impurity of heart that blinds us to God. The divided, scattered, busy, stressed self grows anxious: I cannot see God! If only I could see God I could get all this stuff done and cope better. But it is the pure in heart who can see God. What is the catharsis that is required here? Perhaps some mourning: tears are like a washing out of the self. Perhaps some poverty: having nothing provides a clearing in which God may be noticed. Perhaps fasting, since the Beatitudes are a ladder, so those who hunger and thirst for righteousness are likely to be pure in heart. Perhaps if I could simplify my life I could see God: every day we have thousands of choices, and if over and over we choose the simpler way, if in various ways we choose renunciation, then we are less and less enmeshed in the world, and have more freedom, an available space, a purity so we might see God.

In chapter 13 we will examine the experiences of saints, like Francis of Assisi or Thérèse of Lisieux, who seemed to have overcome their spiritual astigmatism and were able to see God, at least "through a glass, darkly." Near the conclusion of *The City of God*, St. Augustine treated the question of "the kind of vision with which the saints will see God, in the world to come."[9] Now, at best, because of our fallen nature, our impurity of heart, if we see God we see through that "glass, darkly" (even for a spiritual hero like Paul). But it will not always be so: "When the body, freed from corruption, offers no hindrance to the soul, the saints will certainly need no bodily eyes to see what is there to be seen." On the last page of *The City of God*, Augustine beautifully framed the future of the pure in heart as "the Lord's Day . . . which is to last forever. . . . There we shall be still and see; we shall see and we shall love; we shall love and we shall praise. Behold, what will be, in the end, without end!"[10] The pure in heart see, and they see in order to love, and they love to fulfill their eternal vocation of praise. Such is Jesus' heady promise.

But we need not wait until heaven dawns to see God, and we need not limit ourselves to a metaphorical kind of seeing in the present. I think the best line in Antoine de Saint-Exupéry's *The Little Prince* is this: "It is only with the heart that one can see rightly; what is essential is invisible to the eye." But many great teachers and heroes, from Gregory of Nyssa in the fourth century to Mother Teresa in the twentieth, have taught us that we "see God" in what is not at all invisible: in our neighbor. Mother Teresa's life was an embodied sermon on Matthew 25:31–46, Jesus' last lesson, in which he intimated we could see his face in the eyes of the poor, hungry, naked, homeless, imprisoned.

> The Missionaries of Charity do firmly believe that they are touching the body of Christ in his distressing disguise whenever they are helping and touching the poor. We cannot do this with a long face.[11]

She spoke on this theme all over the world, and with a pointed urgency.

> At the end of life we will not be judged by how many diplomas we have received, how much money we have made, how many great things we have done. We will be judged by, I was hungry and you gave me to eat, I was naked and you clothed me, I was homeless and you took me in.[12]

The pure in heart love Jesus, and want nothing but to be near him— and so they stick close to the poor Jesus blessed, and so they see him. Blessed are the pure in heart, for they shall see God.

Questions for Discussion

1. Do you find that you "will one thing" in your own life?
2. Do you know people you would characterize as being "pure in heart"? In what ways?
3. Have you seen instances where love has obliterated the difficulties of circumstances? When?

Peacemakers

Blessed are the peacemakers.

—Matthew 5:9

Jesus does not say, "Blessed are those who *have* peace,"[1] although we come to God longing for some peace in our hearts. Jesus does not say, "Blessed are those who prefer peace, wish for peace, await peace, love peace, or praise peace,"[2] however fond we may be of peace. Jesus says, "Blessed are the peace-makers—those who make peace." The Greek word *eirēnopoioi* means, literally, "doers of peace" or "makers of peace."

In response to a sermon in which I spoke about Jesus and his apparent obsession with peace, and the implications of his zeal for peacemaking in our world today, a parishioner e-mailed me, explaining how boneheaded and irresponsible "passivism" is. Now perhaps what I saw on the computer screen was nothing more than a spelling error, but I suspected (rightly) that this person, who is hardly alone, thought of "pacifism" as "passivism," that somehow "peace" suggests that we do absolutely nothing, that we be passive in the face of evil. Nothing could be further from the truth. Jesus said, "Blessed are the doers of peace, the makers of peace." To do peace, to make peace, you have to get busy, you have to act, you have a world of work ahead of you.

Naming Peace

But what is the nature of this work? As a minimum, we have to think and talk about peace. The dark lord in the *Harry Potter* books is so evil that he is known as "he who must not be named." Today, in the post-9/11 world, our thinking has hardened into such steely, abject ugliness that "peace" is the name that apparently must not be spoken. Candidates dare not utter the word. Proponents of war (in either party) could conceivably speak zealously for "peace," but do not. Even in church, among us who claim to serve the Prince of Peace, it is hard to scare up a conversation about "peace." We speak only of politics, victory, our safety.

As the first Gulf War opened in 1991, three clergy were interviewed on the *McNeill-Lehrer Hour*. Two declared, "God is with us, we must win!" The third opened his Bible and read aloud about Jesus: "Love your enemies." "Blessed are the peacemakers . . ." and was interrupted by a shout from the man next to him: "That's not relevant now! We're at war!" His reply? "If it's not relevant now, it's never relevant."

Once upon a time, peacemaking was an honorable vocation. But now all we know is force. The inhabitants of Jesus' world knew a bogus kind of peace. Caesar Augustus boasted of countless achievements, the grandest being the *pax romana*, the peace that slammed down over the empire during his reign. But Augustus's peace was a chimera, faked because he had enough swords to point at citizens and slaves. Peace is not the absence of war, especially when war is shoved aside by bullying threats. Incidentally, this applies not only on the international stage, but also in your home. If dad shouts and waves a mighty fist, and his wife and children cower silently, there is no peace in that home.

Genuine peace is deeper, richer, giving life to those in the home and in the world, letting them be free to be the people God made them to be, participating, interacting, not fearful but joyful, not walking on eggshells but dancing in the streets. The Old Testament vision of peace, of *shalom*, is all about the well-being of God's people, of *all* God's people, from the richest to the poorest, from the most agile to the lame, from the brilliant to the slow of mind. *Shalom* is about justice, living out the truth of God's kingdom.

Truth and Justice

How do peacemakers make peace? How do we think about peace? Peace is not doing nothing. Peace labors long and hard, and we begin by *thinking*. Hitler once said to his henchmen in the Reichstag, "It is fortunate for leaders when the people do not think." Blessed are those who think, and especially those who think of peace.

Dietrich Bonhoeffer said, "There can only be . . . peace when it does not rest on lies and injustice."[3] To get close to Jesus, we have to be adamant about telling the *truth*. We have gotten so accustomed to lies and half-truths, to spin and ideology, that we do not even expect truth. I read George Orwell's *1984* in the 1960s; it felt futuristic, portraying what might happen if we lose our minds as a society. My daughter read it twenty years after 1984, and its words indict us as actually having lost our minds: the "Ministry of Truth" declares that "War is peace, Ignorance is strength, Lies become truth; every year our range of consciousness grows a little smaller."

Peacemakers stare truth in the face and do not flinch, and then they dare to repeat it. People suffer in our world, and in our homes. There is a history to the world, and in our families. The carnage of conflict ruins the precious image of God in the peoples of the world, and in the person overhearing a heated argument in the kitchen. With profound wisdom and uncommon courage, South African leaders determined that the only way to move forward in the post-apartheid era would be to form a "Truth and Reconciliation" commission. All over South Africa, victims and perpetrators told their stories; women faced policemen who had murdered their husbands and children and told of their agony. Henchmen who carried out vile orders admitted their guilt. Justice was meted out, and yet the most astonishing moments of reconciliation, which would strike many of us as implausible, happened—because the truth simply had its day out in the open.

We may disagree about the answer to Pilate's question "What is truth?" Within the church we do not have much peace, as we are riddled with division on so many issues that matter. Our society is rife with rancor, and we view the guy down the street as a numskull because of the political sign in his yard. We have forgotten how to disagree. In a democracy, we ought to be able to disagree and not shoot each other. We can thrash through issues, listen, learn, test out our ideas, understand why others think as they do. "Learning how to disagree" sounds like making peace, and is also the secret of inching ever closer to the truth, without which we will never have any peace.

I see bumper stickers around town that say "No Justice, No Peace." Injustice poisons any kind of superficial peace. The biblical vision of *shalom* presumes *justice*—and we may notice with some curiosity how the Old Testament defined "justice." The Hebrew, *mishpat*, is not about the good being rewarded and the bad being punished. *Mishpat* is not about fairness to the individual, but rather health to the community. *Mishpat* dawns when the poorest in a community are cared for. Do you want to know if a community or nation is just? Just ask if the neediest are cared for.

Of course, part of the "care" a community must exercise is taking evil and sin into account and dealing with it appropriately. Peace does not mean leaving evildoers on the loose. Peace is not passive, but aggressive, engaging in the far more arduous labor of making peace, of reconciling with the person who hates you, of sparing no effort to get inside the other's skin and figuring out how to live together on this planet. But the dominant melody in the chorus of justice is one of care, of inclusion, of striving after *shalom*. Peacemaking requires people who work tirelessly for a just society that mirrors, however obliquely, the kingdom of God.

The Shifting of Power

This is why peacemaking is so arduous, and why it thrusts us into inevitable conflict. Can we sense the irony in Jesus' words? "I have not come to bring peace, but a sword" (Matt. 10:34). Of course he came to bring peace, and he never toted or wielded a sword—to the disappointment of many who felt he was the man to lead an armed revolt against Rome. His metaphorical sword cut through the values and sinful arrangements of the world he found, and of every world that would ever occupy this planet; his teaching and suffering raise question marks against the status quo in every time and place, and against superficial, self-indulgent misunderstandings of what peace is about. Jim Forest tells the sad truth: "Unfortunately, for most of us peace is not the kingdom of God but a slightly improved version of the world we already have. We would like to get rid of conflict without eliminating the factors, spiritual and material, that create division."[4]

For peace to be made, anywhere, anytime, some shift in *power* relationships must happen. For a tall, muscular guy with a twenty-inch iron sword to be at peace with a little, scrawny guy with a pebble in his hand, the big guy has to relinquish his bigness, he has to decide not to tower in intimidation; and the little guy has to decide not to run, and not to be a sneaky guerilla from jealousy over the big guy's sword. When the strong befriend the weak, dignity and strength are imparted to the weak—although, in reality, dignity and strength flow both ways, don't they? All this makes complete sense if we think of the Beatitudes as a ladder. For who is more able, more eager, more willing to make peace than the poor? Or those who mourn (who see through tears the futility of fighting)? Or the meek (who have no turf to protect)? Or the merciful (who embrace forgiveness)? Or the pure in heart (who want only one thing and don't get distracted)?

Peacemaking seems almost impossibly daunting—but largely because we do not think so much about making peace until war is raging. What if we thought of peacemaking less as a remedy, and more as a preventative? Haven't we failed to work on peace when there is *not* conflict? To bring it up once we're in the thick of war is like suggesting to an enraged married couple that they might work on tender communication but the pots and pans are already flying.

As we have noticed, peace within the home is not so very different from peace on the international stage—and, oddly enough, the linchpin for both is *love*. Jesus said, "Love your enemies." Jesus said, "Love your neighbor," and illustrated what he meant with one of his best stories: a Samaritan picks up the person he dreads the most, a Jew; he loves the unlovable one. He makes peace, and does so with concrete, risky but healing actions. Martin Luther King Jr. understood the heart of this Beatitude:

> Love is the only force capable of transforming an enemy into a friend. We never get rid of an enemy by meeting hate with hate; we get rid of an enemy by getting rid of enmity. By its very nature, hate destroys and tears down; by its very nature, love creates and builds up.[5]

God loves us, and transforms our enemies into God's friends, and so we have little choice but to get rid of our enemies and build up new friends. Love is the reason violence cannot deliver the peace it may promise. Bonhoeffer understood the blessed peacemakers:

They renounce all violence. . . . In the case of Christ nothing is to be gained by such methods. His kingdom is one of peace. . . . His disciples keep the peace by choosing to endure suffering themselves rather than inflict it on others. They overcome evil with good, and establish the peace of God in the midst of a world of war and hate.[6]

Love just cannot bring itself to lash out, to strike the beloved.

Forgiveness

So we find ourselves headed toward a new wrinkle in peacemaking. In the same sermon in which Bonhoeffer declared "truth" as the basis of peace, he added, "The forgiveness of sins still remains the sole ground of all peace."[7] We may do a lot of pretending, or we may "kiss and make up" in the home to try to regain peace, when our real need is to dive into the thicket of the issue and try to understand, acknowledge, strategize, and mostly to forgive. We may shrink back from forgiveness, from the making of peace, not merely because it's hard work, but because there can be something darkly delicious about an unhealed grievance.

To lick your wounds, to smack your lips over grievances long past, to roll over your tongue the prospect of bitter confrontations still to come, to savor to the last toothsome morsel both the pain you are given and the pain you are giving back—in many ways, it is a feast fit for a king. The chief drawback is that what you are wolfing down is yourself. The skeleton at the end of the feast is you. (Frederick Buechner)[8]

Unforgiven sin between us tangles us up in some barbed wire that lacerates the soul. This is hard, and countercultural, for we live in a society of blame. Politicians know whom to blame; couples wrangle and blame the flawed spouse; institutions get blamed for all evils; citizens leap into court to blame someone for something. But the Gospel would liberate us from the steel trap of blame. In John Irving's *The World According to Garp*, Helen and Garp have wounded each other in unspeakable ways (actually, they are literally unable to speak because of injuries incurred in an accident). Garp, after days of raging silence, takes a slip of paper, scribbles on it, and hands it to his estranged wife: "I don't blame you." After a while, he hands her another slip: "I don't blame me either." And then a third: "Only in this way can we be whole again."[9]

Forgiveness isn't always a warm, fuzzy feeling. If you forgive me, it doesn't mean you feel like showering me with hugs and kisses. Forgiveness is a decision, a commitment to look at me through God's eyes, to stick with me. In broken families, this is a daunting challenge: you may forgive a parent, or a spouse, but this does not require one ounce of gushy emotion. Forgiveness is not just a word, not just a feeling, but a behavior, a practice, a new habit of behavior whose goal is nothing less than a fully restored relationship.

Forgiveness, making peace, is like putting on some new spectacles that correct our cloudy vision. In the comedy film *Bruce Almighty*, the insensitive, knuckleheaded Bruce is finally broken down by life, brokenhearted over squandering his relationship with Grace—and in his humbled misery finds himself face to face with God, who asks, "What do you really want, Bruce? Do you want Grace back?" Bruce, finally understanding, surprises even God by saying, "No. I want her to meet somebody who will love her, who will give her what she deserved from me. I want her to meet someone who will see her the way I see her now—through your eyes."

Blessed are the peacemakers. They see other people through God's eyes. And not just the people up close, across the dining room table. We mean *all* people. However repulsive the thought may be, all that we have said in the last six or seven paragraphs applies not just to "relationships," but also among nations. There will never be peace on this earth, there will never be peace between any two warring nations, there will never be peace between bands of people who hate each other, until there is forgiveness. No politician will nail "forgiveness" as the primary plank of his policy platform! But be very sure: the forgiveness of peacemaking is the heart of Jesus' mission. "Blessed are the peacemakers." Why would Jesus care about the people we despise? Or for us, for that matter? And why are peacemakers blessed? How did Jesus finish this Beatitude?

"For They Shall Be Called 'Sons of God'"

When Martin Luther King Jr. waxed eloquent about his "dream" (which is God's dream) on the steps of the Lincoln Memorial in August of 1963, his most compelling image was of "little black boys and black girls . . . able to join hands with little white boys and white girls as sisters and brothers."[10] Children, with no genetically endowed hatred for each other, not yet jaded by prejudice or suspicion: peacemaking, in Jesus' kingdom, is all about the daughters and sons of God. In the community Jesus came to create (or rather, to help us notice is already there!), we are a family, however trite the image has become. Perhaps the fact that we are family goes a long way toward explaining why we have such difficulty getting along, and why so much peacemaking is needed!

Clarence Jordan noticed a fascinating connection between this Beatitude about peacemakers as sons and daughters of God and that moment in John's Gospel when Jesus speaks with Nicodemus about the "new birth," being "born again." What does it mean to be in God's family?

> Though Matthew does not use the term "the new birth," the Beatitudes seem to be a detailed explanation of it. And while John does not give the Beatitudes, the figure of birth is apparently used to illustrate them. Whether we call the process Beatitudes or birth, the result is the same: "sons of God." Both accounts agree that sonship is a basic requirement for membership in God's family.[11]

To discover your identity in the family of God, to be a sibling to Jesus, who said, "Blessed are the peacemakers, for they shall be called sons of God," we dispense with the world's conventional wisdom to "play it safe," to "just get along," and we exhibit our relatedness by making peace in God's world. Jesus was sized up by the Romans as a threat to peace. His followers "disturbed the peace" in Philippi, Thessalonica, and Ephesus (Acts 16–19), and have continued to do so in virtually every age and place. They look like troublemakers; but actually they are glued to Jesus in real life.

> Jesus, the Prince of Peace, and Son of God, calls those who work for peace his brothers and sisters. Those who stand in a divided

world, pointing the way to unity; those who live in a hateful world, demonstrating the way of love; those who share with Jesus the ministry of reconciliation; these are the people most closely related to him.[12]

Peter Storey spoke these words in 1976 at a commitment service for the South African Council of Churches on a Sunday. By Wednesday, bullets were flying in Soweto; nearly six hundred children and youth were killed. So it goes for peacemakers, who look like troublemakers to those who cannot see Jesus' kingdom. And so we lean in to the last Beatitude, the grim one that reminds us the going won't be easy, the realistic one that braces us for the future, the tragic one that sweeps off the table any notion that the Beatitudes are about "being happy," as the world so trivially imagines being happy.

Questions for Discussion

1. In what ways is "peace" more than just "passivism" or the absence of war?
2. Where do you see instances of the relationship of "justice" and "peace"?
3. What are ways in which you perceive your identity as a "child of God" to be related to being a "peacemaker"?

12

Persecuted

Blessed are those who are persecuted for righteousness' sake, for theirs is the kingdom of heaven. Blessed are you when men revile you and persecute you and utter all kinds of evil against you falsely on my account. Rejoice and be glad, for your reward is great in heaven, for so men persecuted the prophets who were before you.

—Matthew 5:10–12

*I*n our study so far, the Beatitudes have been a series of repeated mental jolts to the way we usually think about the world, and yet the seven are nonetheless comforting, and also hopeful. But with number eight, we begin to realize that Jesus is not just a man with strange views. He is not just odd, but downright dangerous, and those in proximity to him will likely be in peril as well.

And his listeners have no choice but to take this personally. While on the subject of the meek or the peacemakers, he spoke in the third person, so he might have meant somebody else. But now he looks them directly in the eyes and shifts to the second person—"Blessed are *you*"—which would be welcome, had he not continued with "when people revile you and persecute you." So, as if sensitive to the dangers and actual harm his followers would face, and the questions they would harbor, Jesus lingers, adding to the eighth a ninth beatitude, longer than the others, eight and nine really collapsing into a single, more patient, somber counsel.

Jesus does not say *if* you are reviled and persecuted, but *when* you are reviled and persecuted. The word *dediogmenoi* ("persecuted") implies verbal or physical abuse (or both); and the verbal form is the perfect tense, intimating that this persecution is a fact of the past, which endures into the present. Certainly, when Jesus said what he said, the disciples probably scratched their heads and wondered what it could mean; the crowd was probably more confused, still scrambling to catch up with the earlier Beatitudes.

But one generation later, the readers of Matthew's Gospel knew. By the time Matthew wrote down what Jesus said, verbal abuse was flying, many connected to the fledgling Christian movement had suffered physical harm, and the danger was mounting.[1] John the Baptist had been beheaded. Jesus was gruesomely crucified. Stephen, whose face shone like an angel, was the first to lose his life because of Christ, stoned by a surging mob that included Saul, who later became Paul (Acts 6:8–8:1). Herod Agrippa had James, the brother of John, killed by the sword (Acts 12:2).

Paul and Silas arrived in Philippi and preached—and were summarily thrown in jail for "disturbing our city" (Acts 16:20). Incarcerated in pitch-black darkness, beaten with rods, and shackled in stocks, instead of weeping and screaming for help Paul and Silas were singing hymns. Did they know Jesus had said, "Rejoice and be glad"? Paul eventually made it to Rome, where he was executed around the year 64. So was Peter, to whom Jesus had sternly explained, "Whoever would save his life will lose it, and whoever loses his life for my sake will find it" (Matt. 16:25). Perhaps Peter understood years later, for the New Testament letter bearing his name says, "If you do suffer for righteousness' sake, you will be blessed" (1 Pet. 3:14).

Jews like Jesus and the disciples were reared on stories of persecution. Jesus alluded to the long history of God's servants' being assaulted by the powers that be when, at the crest of the Mount of Olives, with its panoramic view of the city, he lamented, "O Jerusalem, Jerusalem, killing the prophets and stoning those who are sent to you!" (Matt. 23:37) —and he had many such prophets in mind. Little-known Zechariah was killed by King Joash (2 Chron. 24:21). Isaiah, according to tradition, fled for the hills outside Jerusalem, but the henchmen of wicked King Manasseh tracked him down and sawed him in two (Heb. 11:37). During the days of Jeremiah, another prophet, Uriah, was executed by King Jehoiakim (Jer. 26:23). Jeremiah himself was ridiculed and imprisoned, and many believed he was stoned to death in Egypt, so pointed was his continuing protest against idolatry. From the spot where he was standing, Jesus could see three stunning rock-hewn monuments on the eastern slope of the Kidron Valley. All Jews were familiar with these "tombs of the prophets," particularly the square stone tomb with a pyramid-shaped roof known as Zechariah's tomb; and another the so-called tomb of Jason.

"Rejoice and Be Glad?"

So we can only imagine the nervous glances exchanged, the shuffling of feet, when Jesus said, "Rejoice and be glad, for your reward is great in heaven, for so men persecuted the prophets who were before you." Why rejoice and be glad? Because you will find yourselves in impressive company? Why had there been, and why would there be, such a hostile reaction to God's message?

Truth always has a way of clashing with the status quo, with the vested patterns of sinful behavior in which even religious people get stuck. Certainly, Christianity was a cultural revolution. Remember what Christianity's opponents blurted out in Thessalonica? "'These [people] who have turned the world upside down have come here also, and . . . they are all acting against the decrees of Caesar, saying that there is another king, Jesus'" (Acts 17:6–7). Caesar brooked no competition from fools who bowed before Jesus as "king." Some Christians were executed for such nonsense; others suffered more routine difficulties, like ostracism, the loss of business contacts, being the butt of jokes, never getting invited to a party.

Over time, Christians increasingly felt the harsh steel of Roman oppression. The emperor Nero, looking for scapegoats after Rome burned, tarred Christians and burned them as torches to light his garden. The intensity of persecution grew white-hot in the years after Matthew was written. By the second century, onlookers were puzzled and hostile. Minucius Felix described Christians as "a tribe obscure, shunning the light, dumb in public though talkative in the corners."[2] Their radical faith, their ethical determination, their refusal to knuckle under before the powers that be put them at odds with business, religious, and political leaders, and even with friends and family. At the same time, their secretive nature led to misunderstanding of who they were and what they did. Suspicious critics, knowing only enough of the truth to see it as dangerous, accused them of cannibalism, drinking blood, ritual murder, or promiscuous intercourse. Most importantly and not at all erroneously, they were labeled as unpatriotic, easy targets because of their peaceful and unarmed ways.

And so hundreds of men, women, and children, were killed. Byron surveyed the Colosseum in Rome and said, "Heroes have trod this spot,"[3] noting how Christians were forced to fight as gladiators, and were thrown to wild beasts. We have the detailed correspondence of Pliny to the emperor Trajan regarding how to handle dissident Christians. Showing them statues of the emperor and the Capitoline gods (Jupiter, Juno, and Minerva), Pliny would demand a sacrificial offering and verbal denial of Christ. Some recanted and were spared, although Pliny observed that "real Christians" could not be forced to do so. Countless martyrs preferred death to renouncing their faith.

Ironically, persecution fueled the rapid growth of the church. Tertullian wrote that "the blood of the martyrs is the seed of the church."[4] And it was not merely that they died, but rather the *way* they died. When the bishop of Smyrna, Polycarp, was burned at the stake in the year 156, he refused to curse Christ, saying:

> Eighty-six years have I served him, and he has done me no wrong; how could I blaspheme my king who saved me? You threaten the fire that burns for an hour, but then is quenched; you are ignorant of the fire of judgment to come. Why delay? Do what you wish.[5]

Onlookers, including the proconsul, were awed by the joy and peace on his face, even as he perished in the flames. As he breathed his last, did he recall that Jesus had said, "Blessed are those who are persecuted for righteousness' sake. . . . Rejoice and be glad, for your reward is great in heaven, for so men persecuted the prophets who were before you"?

The Cost of Discipleship

And so it has always been, at least when Christians have been serious about following Christ. Mind you, there has always existed a tame, bland version of Christianity, watered down sufficiently to be able to fit in and get along. G. K. Chesterton quotably said, "The Christian ideal has not been tried and found wanting; it has been found difficult and left untried."[6] When real Christianity has been tried, it has proven to be difficult. It bumps up against the ways of the world; points of conflict pierce serious believers. While many are familiar with Bonhoeffer's duly famous book *The Cost of Discipleship*, we may overlook the fact that he was writing on the Sermon on the Mount, and specifically its opening, the "blessed" life of the Beatitudes:

> Cheap grace is grace without discipleship, grace without the cross, grace without Jesus Christ, living and incarnate. Costly grace is the treasure hidden in the field; for the sake of it, a man will gladly go and sell all that he has. It is the pearl of great price, it is the rule of Christ, for whose sake a man will pluck out the eye which causes him to stumble, it is the call of Jesus at which the disciple leaves his nets and follows him. Costly grace is the gospel which must be sought again and again. Such grace is *costly* because it calls us to follow, and it is *grace* because it calls us to follow Jesus Christ. It is costly because it costs a man his life, and it is grace because it gives a man the only true life. Above all, it is costly because it cost God the life of his Son.[7]

If his faithful commitment to the God he called "Abba" cost Jesus his life, why should following him be comfortable and pain-free? Why would we expect to find ourselves in sync with a world that is so out of sync with God? As we sort through what the Beatitudes mean for us today, we need to pause, take a deep breath, and reflect on the truth: if we absorb Jesus' words, if we walk in his way, if we try to embody his words and stick closely to him in the real world, we will suffer.

One form of that suffering is especially problematical for us can-do Americans: we probably will fail. No, we *will* fail. Much of what we do will seem a total waste of time. And that will be on the good days. On bad days, we will not only fail to succeed, but we will encounter conflict. We will be reviled and persecuted. What is the old saying—"No good deed goes unpunished"? Discipleship exacts an immense cost on the bad days.

Or are they really bad days? Did Jesus wire the kingdom in such a way that the bad days are really good days? Martin Luther once said, "When the Devil harasses us, we know ourselves to be in good shape."[8] Suffering for Christ is not a signal that we had better change our strategy quickly so all will go smoothly. On the contrary, struggle is evidence we are very near Jesus.

Not that all suffering and difficulty should be laid at Jesus' feet. You are not blessed for failure to pay alimony or for showing up late for work. You are not blessed for a run of seeming bad luck. You may get tangled in difficulties because you didn't plan, or because you were rude. You may stumble because you were self-righteous or spiritually misled. Jesus is careful to say you are blessed when you are reviled and persecuted *for righteousness'* sake, and *on my* account. The question is: Am I suffering because of my conformity to Jesus, or because I am a prickly person? Am I suffering because I look like the kingdom of God? Or is it because I am merely mirroring a conflicted world, but with a charade of faith pasted on the outside?

Something Worth Living For

Jesus says, "Rejoice and be glad. You are stepping into a royal, magnificent stream of tradition when you suffer for being near me. You join hands with Isaiah, Jeremiah, Peter and Paul, saints and martyrs, Mary and her son Jesus." And what Jesus invites us to see is that when we join them, we become people of hope. Hope dawns when we have discovered the pearl of great price, the one true path to life. By the time Martin Luther King Jr. marched on Selma in 1965, many had died in the struggle for civil rights. King spoke of the higher value of the truth:

> I can't promise you that it won't get you beaten. I can't promise you that it won't get your home bombed. I can't promise you won't get scarred up a bit—but we must stand up for what is right. If you haven't discovered something that is worth dying for, you haven't found anything worth living for.[9]

This is the often-forgotten plot of the story in Daniel 3. Shadrach, Meshach, and Abednego did not plunge into the fiery furnace with some absolute certainty they would be delivered. They willingly climbed in because their zeal to live for God was more precious than life itself, because they could not tolerate any other god usurping the place of the true God in their lives. Listen to their bold witness:

> "*If* it be so, our God whom we serve is able to deliver us from the burning fiery furnace; and he will deliver us out of your hand, O king. But *if not*, be it known to you, O king, that we will not serve your gods or worship the golden image which you have set up." (Dan. 3:17–18)

God perhaps will save us. But even if God doesn't, we will not compromise, we will not sell our souls to what is not truly God. So valuable is their life with God that even death is preferable to risking the ultimate and eternal good.

For us, even if we are not called upon to sacrifice our lives in some foreign arena, we must weigh the glory God has promised as a vastly richer reward. We are cajoled into bowing down every day before the altar of television, in the corridors of the shopping mall, in the intricacies of our minds, in the thousand little decisions we make hourly. And it is our noble privilege to join the ranks of the martyrs and resolutely declare, "We will not serve your gods or worship the golden image which you have set up"—no matter the cost.

The cost really is only temporary, or even illusory. We may count the cost of non-discipleship—for to miss out on the cost of discipleship is to forsake hope. Many writers have distinguished hope from optimism. Martin Luther King Jr., not long before his assassination, wearied by the travails of the struggles for civil rights, opined, "I am no longer optimistic, but I remain hopeful." This distinction was shrewdly articulated by Christopher Lasch:

> Hope doesn't demand progress; it demands justice, a conviction that wrongs will be made right, that the underlying order of things is not flouted with impunity. Hope appears absurd to those who lack it. We can see why hope serves us better than optimism. Not that it prevents us from expecting the worst; the worst is what the hopeful are prepared for. A blind faith that things will somehow work out for the best furnishes a poor sub-

stitute for the disposition to see things through even when they don't.[10]

The Work of Hope

Hope has noticed that our work extends across time—as King's theological hero Reinhold Niebuhr put it, "Nothing worth doing can be achieved in a single lifetime; therefore we are saved by hope."[11] As people of hope, then, we are liberated from the need for measurable results. I think the Jesus who spoke the Beatitudes would be pleased by this often-quoted letter Thomas Merton wrote to Jim Forest, whose own book on the Beatitudes counsels patience in the face of struggle:

> Do not depend on the hope of results. When you are doing the sort of work you have taken on, essentially an apostolic work, you may have to face the fact that your work will be apparently worthless and even achieve no result at all, if not perhaps results opposite to what you expect. As you get used to this idea, you start more and more to concentrate not on the results, but on the value, the rightness, the truth of the work itself. And there too a great deal has to be gone through, as gradually you struggle less and less for an idea and more and more for specific people. The range tends to narrow down, but it gets much more real. In the end, it is the reality of personal relationships that saves everything. . . . The big results are not in your hands or mine, but they suddenly happen, and we can share in them; but there is no point in building our lives on this personal satisfaction, which may be denied us and which, after all, is not that important. . . . You are probably striving to build yourself an identity in your work, out of your work and your witness. You are using it, so to speak, to protect yourself against nothingness, annihilation. That is not the right use of your work. All the good that you will do will not come from you but from the fact that you have allowed yourself, in the obedience of faith, to be used by God's love. Think of this more, and gradually you will be free from the need to prove yourself, and you can be more open to the power that will work through you without your knowing it. . . . The real hope, then, is not in something we think we can do but in God who is making something good out of it in some way we cannot see. If

we can do His will, we will be helping in this process. But we will not necessarily know all about it beforehand.[12]

These words bear rereading and considerable reflection. We do good, not merely to shield ourselves against meaninglessness, but to be close to Jesus. Once we are fixed on this as our one and only purpose, then we are freed to act faithfully, with a reckless passion that is neither spurred on nor shackled by the actual results obtained. In this final Beatitude, Jesus offers comfort, and the license to press on. Paul understood God's pledge in Jesus:

> Finally, my brethren, rejoice in the Lord. . . . I count everything as loss because of the surpassing worth of knowing Christ Jesus my Lord. For his sake I have suffered the loss of all things, and count them as refuse, in order that I may gain Christ and be found in him, not having a righteousness of my own, based on law, but that which is through faith in Christ, the righteousness from God that depends on faith; that I may know him and the power of his resurrection, and may share his sufferings, becoming like him in his death, that if possible I may attain the resurrection from the dead. . . . I press on toward the goal for the prize of the upward call of God in Christ Jesus. . . . But our commonwealth is in heaven, and from it we await a Savior, the Lord Jesus Christ, who will change our lowly body to be like his glorious body, by the power which enables him even to subject all things to himself. (Phil. 3:1, 8–11, 14, 20–21)

"Blessed are . . . [the] persecuted. . . . Rejoice and be glad, for your reward is great in heaven." The Beatitudes as a whole, and their haunting conclusion in particular, reveal that our true identity is not defined by what transpires on this earth, and is not limited to what we see here and now. We are transitory pilgrims passing through this place, headed toward a distant destination we cannot even see clearly, but a future in which we can trust fervently.

Notice Jesus provides not the slightest solace that the difficulties his followers will face are about to ease up or will pass quickly so we might return to a comfortable life. The tribulation of following Christ in the real world didn't ease up for the disciples, or for Jesus, just as they hadn't for "the prophets who were before you." We may recall God's far from comforting reply to Jeremiah, when the prophet groaned under the weight of all he was suffering in the cause of speaking out for God in an Israel that had lost its theological mind. Tormented by his compulsion he cries out, "Why do the wicked prosper? How long, O Lord?"—to which God answers, "If you have raced with men on foot, and they have wearied you, how will you compete with horses? And if in a safe land you fall down, how will you do in the jungle of the Jordan?" (Jer. 12:5).

Those who are confident in God's future gallop as best they can with those horses, and keep picking themselves up no matter how often (or harshly) they are thrown down. On the wall of Shishu Bhavan, a children's home in Calcutta operated by Mother Teresa's order, the Sisters of Charity, are these words, which capture the heart of all the Beatitudes as brought into focus by the last Beatitude:

> People are unreasonable, illogical, and self-centered.
> Love them anyway.
> If you do good, people will accuse you of selfish, ulterior
>   motives.
> Do good anyway.
> If you are successful, you win false friends and true enemies.
> Succeed anyway.
> The good you do will be forgotten tomorrow.
> Do good anyway.
> Honesty and frankness make you vulnerable.
> Be honest and frank anyway.
> What you spent years building may be destroyed overnight.
> Build anyway.
> People really need help but may attack you if you help them.
> Help people anyway.
> Give the world the best you have and you'll get kicked in the
>   teeth.
> Give the world the best you've got anyway.[13]

Having reached the end of the Beatitudes, we may ask for evidence that any of this really happens in human life—and plenty of evidence is at hand.

Questions for Discussion

1. Have you personally experienced being "persecuted for right-eousness' sake" or been reviled or had "all kinds of evil" spoken against you because of Christ? Why or why not? When and how?
2. What is the difference between "optimism" and "hope"?
3. In what ways does being "people of hope" liberate us to take the risks for persecution and suffering?

Now faith is the assurance of things hoped for, the conviction of things not seen. Heb 11:1

13

Saints and Heroes

Jesus did not talk so that his words might be etched in the hall of fame of shrewd sayings. Jesus spoke to draw people around him, to light some fire in them, to get them in motion, active in the world, to be the people about whom onlookers would say, "These [people] who have turned the world upside down have come here also."

We never understand the Beatitudes if we merely read a book like this one, or if we sit around a comfortable Sunday-school-room table and talk about them with others who are like us. Nicholas Lash helpfully framed the issue by saying that the Scriptures are like a script to be "performed."[1] Just as a musical score does not exist merely to be studied at someone's class-room desk, but is intended for the musicians who are to pick up their instruments and perform the work together, so the Scriptures exist for us as the people of God to embody the words in the real world. We will follow Christ in clumsy, awkward ways. But then Jesus didn't commend the stellar or the formidable, but the meek, those who hunger and thirst for righteousness, not those who possess it.

If the church is to make a difference in the world, we should start with these Beatitudes, remembering that our persuasiveness depends upon the degree to which we resemble or at least mirror Jesus.[2] The greatest persuaders the church has ever known, those whom we might mimic if we would ourselves stick close to Christ, are the saints—the officially sanctified saints of the church, but also the unofficial, humble, little-known saints, some of whom we have actually known personally.

Saints have been much talked about, venerated, and occasionally vilified, but it might be helpful to think of the lives of exemplary Christians from the perspective of the Beatitudes. In a sense, the saints are the people who have read the Bible literally—not in the sense of arguing that the world was created in six twenty-four-hour days or that a real whale did in fact swallow Jonah alive, but literally in the sense of thinking, "I am supposed to do this." From St. Francis of Assisi to Clarence Jordan, from St. Anthony to Thérèse of Lisieux, from Dorothy Day to my grandfather, there have always been people who read the Bible and naively interpreted the Scriptures as straightforward directions for living. We may feel we are more sophisticated in our reading of the Scripture, and we may know more about history and nuances of interpretation; but we would be foolish to scoff at the great friends of God who have actually been poor, meek, pure in heart, merciful, peacemakers, and persecuted for their faith.

At first, I thought I would try to imagine one of those dictionaries with a little photograph beside a definition, and to devise an entry for each of the Beatitudes with a picture of the saint who best exemplified poverty, or meekness, or peacemaking. But as soon as I declared one to be poor in spirit, I perceived that she also was merciful; as soon as I pinpointed one as meek, I had to admit that he was also a peacemaker—and got himself killed for his trouble. The Beatitudes truly are a ladder, and the saints teach us that those who are poor in spirit are likely to be hungry for righteousness, that the meek are merciful, that those who mourn make peace, and all of them wind up a laughingstock in a world that does not value holiness.

Francis of Assisi

One saint who lived his life rather dramatically on that ladder was Francis of Assisi, and his image could easily be affixed to any of the Beatitudes in our hypothetical dictionary. The robe he wore can be viewed by tourists: it is threadbare, not from the passing of eight centuries, but because Francis gave away the expensive, high-fashion attire of his youth and chose to wear nothing but a quilt of rags sewn together. He chose to be quite literally poor. A young knight, a troubadour, with a fantastic future, shedding everything: Why this lunacy?

Francis was, quite simply, trying to do as Scripture directed, and to be as close to Jesus as possible. He found his possessions got in the way of reaching out to the poor, and that his outward show was mere show, for on the inside we are nothing but poor beggars. So, his poverty of spirit manifested itself in very real poverty. Even when he was offered possessions, he either refused or gave them away immediately, fearing that his energy would be consumed with security and maintaining, instead of with Christ and serving.

The witness of Francis, who was rich yet intentionally became poor, begs for a verdict. Murray Bodo called the poverty of Francis

a divine antidote to the disease which would infect society and, more importantly, the individual, from then on. One's personal value and self-esteem would by and large be measured in proportion to an ability to make money. Money and what it represents becomes the fulness of life. He was the quintessential Christian who saw what money would do to the spirit. Christ alone is the fulness of life, and the compulsive pursuit of money, more than anything else, distracts the individual from what really brings life.[3]

When Francis saw the plight of any creature, human or animal, who suffered, he literally mourned, so much that in the latter stages of his life he had lost most of his vision from so much weeping. He saw the world through tears, and his mourning drew him into action. He was meek, entirely humble. So hungry and thirsty was he for righteousness that he fasted and prayed constantly.

How merciful was Francis? Not only could he not bear for an ant to be stepped on; he cared for every person, even those no one else in Italy would touch. He embraced lepers and all who were shunned. As G. K. Chesterton put it, "Francis had all his life a great liking for people who had been put hopelessly in the wrong." And, setting a standard for us all, Francis "liked those others disliked him for liking."[4]

How pure was his heart? Relentlessly he probed his motives, seeking to be a crystal-clear window into the holy heart of Christ. Once he broke one of his fasts by eating a piece of bread on the thirty-ninth day, anxious that he not be tempted to vainglory.

His peacemaking emerged inevitably from his attitudes of poverty, mourning, mercy, and purity. Francis surprisingly joined a horde of soldiers and knights in the Fifth Crusade in the Middle East. Late in the summer of 1219, the crusaders were arrayed in battle-ready formation at Damietta in Egypt. Francis, barefoot and with no shield or sword, walked bravely across no-man's-land toward the Arab army. The Muslims at first drew their sabers to kill him. But he was so pitiful, so defenseless, so poor, meek, merciful, and pure, that they spared him and led him to the sultan, Malik al-Kamil, who was intrigued with the faith of this misfit soldier. Had it not been for the sultan's fear of his own soldiers, Francis would have pulled off the most unlikely conversion in history. He did manage to secure a little peace in a war-ravaged corner of the globe.

When he learned that a wolf had been terrorizing the village of Gubbio, and that the residents had failed to apprehend him with their knives and nets, Francis (again unarmed) walked up into the hills and found the wolf. He demanded repentance from this creature, but he also noticed that the wolf was painfully hungry, which explained his bad behavior. So he devised a pact with the citizens, who agreed to feed the wolf, who then lived peaceably among them for two years until his death, which was mourned by the people of Gubbio. The miracle, by the way (as Carlo Carretto pointed out), was not that the wolf became tame, but rather that the citizens of Gubbio became tame, "and that they ran to meet the cold and hungry wolf not with pruning knives and hatchets but with bread and hot porridge."[5]

Was Francis persecuted? Interestingly, the fiercest venom unleashed against him personally was from his own father. Pietro Bernardone wanted his son to follow in his footsteps as a businessman dealing in exotic cloth, traveling to great fairs in France, fighting as a knight, rising to the top of society in Umbria. But Francis was summoned on a different adventure. When he began giving his father's precious cloth away to nobodies, Pietro had him locked up, and finally sued him in the city square. Francis, sadly, gave back everything his father had ever given him, including the clothes off his back, and declared publicly, "No longer is Pietro Bernardone my father, but instead my father is 'Our Father, who art in heaven.'" If we are stunned, we have forgotten that the Jesus who said "Blessed are the poor" and "Blessed are you when men persecute you" is the same Jesus who said, "I have come to set a man against his father. . . . He who loves father or mother more than me is not worthy of me" (Matt. 10:35, 37).

Francis had no desire to cleave to Jesus by himself. He was always drawing others, not toward himself, but toward Jesus. Other rich young men in Assisi began throwing it all away, until the town fathers met and concluded some contagion was on the loose. A quarantine was declared, as they hoped to cordon off any spread of such foolishness.

The most foolish, the most delightful, the most blessed of those who joined Francis on his adventure was Brother Juniper. Juniper was deadly serious about imitating Christ, and went at it in a way that showed he grasped the fundamental joy and even mirth of living a holy life. His love for the poor was so great that if he saw someone in need, he would give away the very clothes off his back. Finally his guardian ordered him not to give his tunic, or any part of it, to a beggar.

But soon Juniper was approached by a pauper asking for alms. He replied, "I have nothing to give, except this tunic, and I cannot give it to you due to my vow of obedience. However, if you steal it from me, I will not stop you." Left naked, Juniper returned to the other friars and told them he had been robbed.[6] His compassion became so great that he gave away not only his own things, but the books, altar linens, and capes belonging to other friars. When the poor came to brother Juniper, the other friars would hide their belongings so he could not find them. Rejoice and be glad! Juniper overflowed with joy, as did Francis, whose legacy to us includes poems and songs of praise and sheer delight over the goodness of living in the beautiful theater of God's world, in the closest proximity to Jesus.

"She Must Be a Saint"

But saints who teach us about the Beatitudes are not once-upon-a-time characters captured only in stained glass and fresco. We have photographs and film on quite a few modern saints. At first our minds may gravitate toward someone like Mother Teresa, who gave up a comfortable life to live in solidarity with the poorest of the poor in Calcutta; with holy meekness and a pure heart, she was the very embodiment of mercy, and marshaled a Nobel Peace prize.

Yet, when we think of a Mother Teresa, we often make two mental errors. We may say "Oh, she must be a saint," as if she had some special holiness gene, some superendowment of saintly ability. To say, "She must be a saint" distances us from her and gives us the wiggle room not to go and do likewise. But what Mother Teresa did, any one of us could do. She was neither athletically agile nor an intellectual giant. What she did, picking up a sick child, spooning porridge to a hungry man, smiling, asking others to embrace someone with nothing: I am perfectly capable of doing all these things. If she is a saint, I could be one too.

The second tendency is to think of the saintly as sweet, mild, sugary pastel figures. Some saints have been—but perhaps instead of being a little bored or even put off by sweetness and mildness, we might reconsider these qualities as issuing from blessedness.

Thérèse of Lisieux

Consider Thérèse of Lisieux, who personified the pure heart, the spirit of poverty, a holy meekness, a hunger and thirst for righteousness.[7] In 1877, when Thérèse was four, she loved to dress up as a nun, and repeatedly said her greatest wish was to please Jesus. She was fascinated by saints, and always wished to become one. Having lost her mother, as well as four siblings, she had an eerie longing for heaven, where she might rejoin them. As she grew older, she mourned not only them, but also the slightest sense of separation from Jesus. Frail in health, Thérèse sensed that her own death was never far away.

This keen awareness of the fragility of life wrought in her a remarkable meekness and purity of heart. Above the doorway to her room she carved, "Jesus is my only love." Thérèse exemplified to those around her the cruciality of seemingly trivial, small acts of love. She called it "the little way," partly indicating the simple deeds of love that are the life of holiness, and also embodying the profound theological truth that God's power is revealed in our meekness. When no one would work with Sister Marie in the linen room, so fierce was her anger, Thérèse volunteered and was merciful. Her sister Leonie once remarked that she had never seen Thérèse looking in a mirror. Moments before her death at age 24, she clutched her crucifix to her body and said, "Oh, I love you." She opened her eyes widely, looking straight up, making those near her believe it was her first clear glimpse into the kingdom of God. The year was 1897, the same year Dorothy Day (who would write a beautiful book about Thérèse) was born.

Dorothy Day

If Thérèse seems sweet, Dorothy Day does not, reminding us that many of those Jesus would pronounce as blessed are not bland characters. Some are rather crusty, with jagged edges, anything but syrupy. Consider Dorothy Day. I know of not a single photo of her in which she conveys a hint of sweetness.[8] She lived a rough, dog-eared life, battling inner crises and what she called the "long loneliness." In childhood photos, she appears serious, prematurely grown-up. When she was eight, she was in the thick of the San Francisco earthquake. Later she remembered that "while the crisis lasted, people loved each other. It was as though they were united in Christian solidarity. It makes one think of how people could, if they would, care for each other in times of stress, unjudgingly in pity and love." That loving solidarity provided the script for her life.

As a young adult, she abandoned her childhood religion. Only after an abortion, a divorce, and a child born out of wedlock did she return to the church for which she had little patience, where she had seen people fawn over the rich but do nothing for the poor. Fortunately for us she came back anyway, as a missionary from the streets into the church, worrying that she was being untrue to the poor she loved, yet determined to remind the church that it does in fact have a social program.

She became poor, and not merely in spirit. Her mourning manifested itself as prophetic rage as she published a newspaper out of her own kitchen, selling *The Catholic Worker* for a penny a copy, cheap enough for anyone to buy and read. She challenged the laziness of an uninvolved church that ignored Christ's mandate to care for the poor. She questioned how the church could bless the powers that be, instead of lifting up the powerless. She tackled racism and unfairness in the workplace. The church did not always appreciate being told the truth about its calling. But despite the contempt of church authorities, circulation of her paper skyrocketed from a first-edition run of 2,500 to more than 150,000 in three years.

She made peace and exercised unmatched mercy. She personally opened dozens of shelters (the first was her own apartment, which also housed the paper!), places where the poor could come to eat, pray, make friends, and get vocational training. No one preached at them. They were simply loved and welcomed. Hospitality was everything: "Let's all try to be poorer. My mother used to say, 'Everyone take less, and there will be room for one more.' There was always room for one more at our table."[9] The sorrow and loneliness of her own life sharpened her sensitivity to those who were lonely and sorrowful. The answer to her own plight was the answer to the plight of those to whom she reached out.

> The only answer in this life, to the loneliness we are all bound to feel, is community. The living together, working together, sharing together, loving God and loving our brother, and living close to him in community so we can show our love for him.[10]

For community to happen, we must recognize the dignity of the poor, whom Jesus declared "blessed." One day, a well-dressed woman visited Dorothy Day and donated a diamond ring. Dorothy thanked her, and later in the day gave the ring to an elderly woman who took most of her meals at the shelter. A coworker protested, suggesting Dorothy should have sold the ring and used the money to pay the woman's rent for a year. But Dorothy insisted that the woman have her dignity. The woman could choose what to do with the ring. She could pay her rent for a year; or she could just wear the ring, like the woman who donated it. "Do you suppose that God created diamonds only for the rich?"[11]

The Blessed Farther South

She was persecuted, arrested frequently, and reviled in the press, and seemed to enjoy it. One night she was visiting a friend down in Georgia and got shot at by the KKK. The friend was Clarence Jordan, another not-so-serene saint whom we may take as illustrative of the

Beatitudes. Jordan wrote saucily about the Beatitudes, and we have quoted him several times in this book. But more compellingly, he lived out its words. His poverty of spirit led him to live on a commune-style farm, as his meekness led him to obey what the Bible suggested about Christians sharing their possessions in common (Acts 2 and 4). He mourned a racially divided Georgia, and was incessantly threatened and harassed by the Klan.

The making of peace is hard work, and just west of Jordan's farm a petite Methodist seamstress, Rosa Parks, humbly exhibited a holy meekness that shifted the world's axis just a little. On December 1, 1955, she climbed on a city bus with a handful of others, to go home after a long day at work. At a subsequent stop, some white people got on. The driver, J. P. Blake, did what all drivers did, ordering the blacks in the fifth row to yield their seats and move to the back. "Y'all better make it light on yourselves and let me have those seats." Three moved, but Rosa Parks sat, edging snugly against the window. She wasn't trying to make history. She just wanted to go home, and she was just tired of giving in. Two policemen were summoned. She was fingerprinted, and found herself behind bars. She prayed and waited. The authorities in Montgomery did not detain her for long. The spectacle of a humble, harmless woman of forty-two being forcibly restrained was an embarrassment. A month later she lost her job at the department store: peacemakers do get persecuted.

We could fill many chapters with stories of the faithful who have embodied the Beatitudes as a whole, or who have enlightened the heart of a particular Beatitude—such as the Mothers of the Plaza de Mayo, taking to the public square in Argentina to mourn (and protest) the disappearance of their children under a brutal regime; or Dr. Paul Farmer of Harvard, taking to the back roads of rural Haiti to provide health care to the poorest of the poor;[12] or Father Elias Chacour, creating a haven of peace for Jewish, Muslim, Christian, and Druze students in Ibillin in Galilee (where the steps to the new church feature the Beatitudes in multiple languages!);[13] or a persecuted martyr like Archbishop Oscar Romero who denounced the vicious repression of the Salvadoran government, and knew how to be glad in the face of his imminent assassination, as he told a reporter over the telephone:

My life has been threatened many times. I have to confess that as a Christian I do not believe in death without resurrection. If they kill me, I will rise again in the Salvadoran people. . . . God assisted the martyrs and, if necessary, I will feel him very close when I offer him my last breath. More important than the moment of death is giving him all of life and living for him. . . . If God accepts the sacrifice of my life, my hope is that my blood will be like a seed of liberty and a sign that our hopes will soon become reality.[14]

Or the citizens of South Africa, torturers and the tortured, telling their stories and at times showing the most astonishing mercy in the peace-making labors of the Truth and Reconciliation Commission.

Friends and Family

In fact, all of us probably know one of the host of everyday Christians for whom the Beatitudes matter. I buried a good friend and parishioner named Jim White, who daily fixed his attention on a print of the Beatitudes in his bedroom while he lived and then died of cancer. In fact, the Beatitudes have a lovely, poignant relationship with those who have died. One of the lectionary readings for All Saints Day is Matthew 5:1–12. Somehow this text gathers up the virtues that matter, and the closeness to Jesus that would define us.

At his father's funeral, Stanley Hauerwas suggested that this Texas bricklayer was a gentle man.

He did not try to be gentle. . . . That his gentleness was so effort-less helps us better understand Jesus' beatitudes. Too often those characteristics . . . are turned into ideals we must strive to attain. As ideals they can become formulas for power rather than descriptions of the kind of people characteristic of the new age inaugurated by Christ. For the beatitudes are not general recommendations for just anyone but, rather, descriptions of those who have been washed by the blood of the Lamb. Thus, Jesus does not tell us that we should try to be poor in spirit, or meek. . . . We cannot try to be meek and/or gentle in order to become a disciple of this gentle Jesus, but in learning to be his disciples some of us will discover that we have been made gentle. . . . His life was like the beauty he taught me to see in a solid brick wall whose bed joints were uniform and whose head joints true. For the simple gentleness of my father was that which comes to those honed by a craft that gives them a sense of the superior good. My father was incapable of laying brick rough, just as he was incapable of being cruel. It literally hurt him to look at badly done brick work just as it hurt him to see cruelty. Like his gentleness, his sense of craft was also out of step with the spirit of the times. The world wanted work done quickly and cheaply.[15]

Again, the Beatitudes are not eight commandments, but a lovely octagonal gift, the work of God in us, a work that takes time and cannot be finished quickly or cheaply. Bonhoeffer has already taught us much about this slow, sure, and lovely work of God in us, and so when he wrote from his concentration-camp cell, we listen:

We have to learn that personal suffering is a more effective key, a more rewarding principle for exploring the world in thought and action than personal good fortune. We can have abundant life, even though many wishes remain unfulfilled.[16]

And so we look now to the epilogue which, in the nature of everything having to do with Jesus, is the kind of last word that is really the first word.

Questions for Discussion

1. Have you known persons who embody all the Beatitudes? What were they like?
2. In what ways does the witness of Francis of Assisi speak to you and inspire you?
3. Can you name people you believe to be modern-day saints? What are ways that they make the Beatitudes real for others?

Presence of the Future

*A*s we conclude our thinking together about the Beatitudes, we may reflect upon the mysteries of time, suffering, and hope, which together may puzzle us and yet at the same time provide the essential clue to the meaning of our lives. Imagine a middle-school teacher of composition sitting down to grade a paper submitted by a fledgling young writer. She no doubt would circle in red the various tenses, and urge the writer to be consistent, to adopt a single vantage point in time to clean up the composition.

> *Blessed* are *the poor in spirit, for theirs* is *the kingdom of heaven.*
> *Blessed* are *those who mourn, for they* shall be *comforted.*
> *Blessed* are *the meek, for they* shall inherit *the earth.* . . .
> *Blessed* are *those who are persecuted for righteousness' sake, for theirs* is *the kingdom of heaven.* . . .
> *Rejoice and* be glad, *for your reward* is *great in heaven.*

Even that closing sentence: the command, "be glad," indicates something listeners should do now but also tomorrow and in a few centuries, but the present tense, "your reward *is* great in heaven," isn't really a present tense at all, since the heavenly reward *isn't* just yet, but by definition is something that *will* be.

What is Jesus doing? Is he simply sloppy with tenses and moods? As a man with eternity etched on his soul, is time relatively meaningless to him? Or is he trying to tell us something about life with God? Blessedness: Is it out there? Or now? Or somehow both? Or does it dance along the mysterious bridge between the two?

The Feeling of Time

How do we experience time ourselves? Studies indicate that the answer to this depends largely upon who you are and where you find yourself in the pecking order of social standing. The poor, for instance, think almost exclusively about *right now*. Is it cold out? Do I have a blanket? Is there anything to eat? The middle class, who are indoors and are well fed, tend to focus on the *future*. What promotion am I after? How soon can I buy my dream house? I wonder how much we can travel in retirement? The rich, with no need to fret over their future, gaze back upon the *past*: I met grand friends at Woodberry Forest. . . . My grandfather founded this law firm. . . . This desk has been in our family for two centuries.[1]

How did Jesus think about time? And if we are to be near Jesus, if we are to follow Jesus meaningfully, how do we view time? Not as someone who is rich, middle-class, or poor, but as a disciple of Jesus? Perhaps it is fair to say that Jesus lived very much in the present, and yet his mind was riveted on God's apocalyptic future. And the kingdom of God seems to be both.

Or perhaps we might say that Jesus is precisely the point where present and future meet—and we discover in him how they are interwoven, one shaping and informing the other, the two in some vibrant interplay. And the closer we are to Jesus, the closer we are to the future, and thus, at the same time, the closer we are to authentic living in the present. Perhaps that place, Jesus, the crossroads between present and future, is our one true home.

Frederick Buechner wrote that the kingdom of God is "not a place but a condition."

God's kingly will is being done in various odd ways among us even at this moment. . . . Insofar as all the odd ways we do his will at this moment are at best half-baked and halfhearted, the kingdom is still a long way off—a hell of a long way off, to be more precise and theological. As a poet, Jesus is maybe at his best in describing the feeling you get when you glimpse the Thing Itself—the kingship of the king official at last and all the world his coronation. It's like finding a million dollars in a field, he says, or a jewel worth a king's ransom. It's like finding something you

hated to lose and thought you'd never find again—an old keep-
sake, a stray sheep, a missing child. When the kingdom really
comes, it's as if the thing you lost and thought you'd never find
again is you.[2]

Our problem with being in the present is that we do not enjoy unas-
sailable confidence in the future. In fact, the wealthy deceive themselves if they feel utterly secure about their future, for we have a
built-in uncertainty about what might happen next and a congenital
fear of death. We suspect Reynolds Price was right when, on discov-
ering he had a malignant tumor in his spinal cord, he said, "All the
care and cash in the world is a flimsy shield when death comes calling."[3] But then others press toward a trivial, ephemeral future when
possessed by the drive to meet the right person and make the next deal;
and still others are numb if they have stopped caring about the future
altogether.

The Beatitudes reveal what we find elsewhere in the life and teaching of Jesus: that this teacher, this healer from Nazareth, unlike the vast
majority of us mere mortals, seemed fully certain about the future.
Mourning? You will be comforted. Meek? You will inherit the earth.
Hungry? You will be satisfied. Persecuted? You will be rewarded.

The Beatific Vision Then—and Now

In modern times, we are not lacking in viewpoints about heaven. But
sadly, many preachers and writers, striving to titillate us with wonderful thoughts about our heavenly destiny, portray a kind of heaven
that is trivialized, self-indulgent, as if some cashier at the gate of
heaven will pay out on the lottery, and every whim, every craving we
harbor now will be satisfied; as if the best things I have enjoyed in this
life will go on forever, but even better, like a perpetual Thanksgiving
feast, relaxing by the pool, laughing at the perfect party. How shall we
say it? Heaven will not be so vapid.

Ancient theologians understood our future with God far more profoundly. Toward the end of his lengthy tome *The City of God*, Augustine treats the question of how we will see God. Now we merely see
"through a glass darkly, but then we shall see face to face."[4] This

vision "is reserved for us as the reward of faith; and the apostle John speaks of the vision in these words: 'When he is fully revealed, we shall be like him, because we shall see him as he is.'" Our destiny isn't a prolongation of the best we have in this life. In heaven, we quite simply will see God, and we will be made like God.

Heaven has rightly been envisioned as a massive reunion, a marvelous fellowship when we will be reunited with those we have loved and lost, when even those from whom we have been alienated will be reconciled to us. But theologically, the focal point will be on God. Dante imagines himself ultimately finding his way into heaven, where he sees his beloved Beatrice. She glances at him with a smile, but then the two of them turn, together, to praise God forever. Or into more modern times: Thérèse of Lisieux was obsessed with her future in the direct presence of her Lord. Poetry poured from her heart:

> To die of love is what I hope for,
> on fire with his love I want to be,
> to see him, be one with him forever,
> that is my heaven—that's my destiny:
> by love to live.[5]

It was her love and hope that liberated her to be so tender and loving on earth.

Christopher Lasch once wrote that children need to learn about faraway times and places so they can make sense of the world around them.[6] For Christians, the faraway time and place would be heaven, that eschatological future we call the kingdom of God. Our life with God is in the age to come, and yet we participate in that life today. In fact, we miss today if we aren't riveted on the age to come.

The logic is the way Jesus blends his tenses, that the blessed are and will be, that in Jesus future and present become one. So with Augustine, Gregory, Dante, and Thérèse we are fixed on God's future, never missing for one second the marvel that the future orientation of the Beatitudes alters life now: the first half of each Beatitude describes life today; the future promise seeps back into life now, so even those who seem cursed in this world discover the delights of the future already. As we know these words from prayer and worship, our mentality changes; we work to change the world down here.[7]

And not only does our yearning for heaven then deny us any temp-tation toward irresponsibility down here. However awestruck we may be at the prospect of the climactic dawning of God's eternal kingdom, we are thereby also freed to pay attention to how good life actually is down here. Vesting ourselves in God's future does not ruin our appre-ciation of this world; on the contrary, perhaps it is only from that future perspective that we truly see this world clearly for the first time. Christians glibly speak of heaven as "a better place." But contemplate this wisdom from Marilynne Robinson:

> I feel sometimes as if I were a child who opens its eyes on the world and sees amazing things and then has to close its eyes again. I know this is all mere apparition compared to what awaits us, but it is only lovelier for that. There is a human beauty in it. And I can't believe that, when we have all been changed and put on incorruptibility, we will forget our fantastic condi-tion of mortality and impermanence, the great bright dream of procreating and perishing that mean the whole world to us. In eternity this world will be Troy, I believe, and all that has passed here will be the epic of the universe, the ballad they sing in the streets. Because I don't imagine any reality putting this one in the shade entirely, and I think piety forbids me to try.[8]

The Secret of Joy

Finding that intersection of present and future is really a matter of how we see. Jesus, like some theological ophthalmologist, works in us a new way of seeing. We see beyond present reality into God's future, which, although it may be opaque, is not entirely invisible.[9] We detect the hid-den plot running through the various events of history and our lives.

Humbly we realize that often we only grasp that plot in retrospect! When Joseph comes face-to-face with his brothers who had sold him into slavery and broken their father's heart, instead of upbraiding them, he sees the veiled truth: "Do not be distressed . . . because you sold me here; for God sent me before you to preserve life" (Gen. 45:5). And then again, after Jacob had died: "As for you, you meant evil against me, but God meant it for good, to bring it about that many peo-ple should be kept alive, as they are today" (Gen. 50:20). These words characterize exactly what happened to the speaker of the Beatitudes. The meek, pure, merciful peacemaker was persecuted for righteousness' sake; onlookers could see nothing but horror and shame in the cross. But in retrospect we see what God saw, and what perhaps Mary and one or two of those devoted to him may have glimpsed: that his suffering was to be life for us.

The women at the cross wept, as did Joseph when he met his brothers. Blessed are those who mourn—but straining through tears we see clearly the final fruit of the vision Jesus offers: joy. God made us for joy, which is deeper than happiness—yet perhaps joy then is different entirely from happiness and fun. Joy isn't happiness times three, or a really tall stack of fun. Joy makes little sense to onlookers in a culture where advertisers press you incessantly to want more, for joy is already satisfied. Joy is undeterred by circumstance; joy is at peace, for joy knows we are cradled quite securely in God's loving arms. Joy can weather unhappiness. Joy is usually discovered in the middle of sorrow. Suffering is the archaeologist that unearths the treasure of joy. Joy is the candle that flickers in the darkest night.

From one perspective, we choose joy. At each little fork in the road, we can choose joy or choose to be resentful. And yet the very choice of joy is a gift of the Spirit; it is the "fruit" of the Spirit (Gal. 5:22). When joy surprises me, I know I could not have achieved this myself. In fact, sin, pride, and my sense of self-entitlement block out joy. Those blockades must be torn down, by confession, by humility, by a profound sense of gratitude for even the smallest little gift I might have taken for granted five minutes earlier.

All fruit, including joy, requires time, tending, maturing. Evelyn Underhill notes that "it is rather immature to be upset about the weather. . . . Pursuing the spiritual course, we must expect fog, cold, persistent cloudiness, gales, and sudden stinging hail, as well as the sun."[10] Joy is constant. Joy is consistency in the spiritual life. Joy does not evaporate when God seems absent. Joy trusts God, not emotion, and never falls for the lie that God might just drift away. The very fact that we turn our heads and grope after God in the dark is God's gift that gives birth to joy.

Joy is always elusive, at least while our feet walk about on the earth. We taste joy, but the very taste whets our appetite for more.

C. S. Lewis defined joy as "an unsatisfied desire which is itself more desirable than any other satisfaction."[11] We live in this in-between zone defined by 1 Peter 1:6–8:

> In this you rejoice, though now for a little while you may have to suffer various trials, so that the genuineness of your faith, more precious than gold which though perishable is tested by fire, may redound to praise . . . of Jesus Christ. Without having seen him you love him; . . . you believe in him and rejoice with unutterable and exalted joy.

It is this Jesus who says, "Rejoice and be glad." Joy is the fruit of the Spirit, a gift—as is the life portrayed by Jesus in the Beatitudes. And so we wade into the water, almost as novices who never learned to swim. At first, the nonswimmer experiences the water as the enemy, as all peril. He flails, struggles mightily, feeling his body sinking, unable to battle the water successfully to stay afloat. But a loving instructor looks him in the eye and says: "Trust the water. Don't fight the water. Just rest, be still. The water will hold you." And so, gradually, the nonswimmer relaxes, and discovers to his surprise a buoyancy. And then he is no longer a nonswimmer. Trust the Spirit. Trust the speaker of the Beatitudes. And then you will be blessed.

Questions for Discussion

1. In what ways would you describe the Beatitudes as bringing together the "present" and the "future"?
2. How does the perspective of faith help us recognize the realities of which the Beatitudes speak?
3. In what ways has this study of the Beatitudes increased your joy and encouraged you to live as Jesus taught?

Notes

Chapter 1: What Jesus Didn't Say

1. Plato, *Gorgias* 431b.
2. William Butler Yates, "The Second Coming."
3. Allen Verhey, *Remembering Jesus: Christian Community, Scripture and the Moral Life* (Grand Rapids: Wm. B. Eerdmans Publishing Co., 2002), 249.
4. David Brooks, *On Paradise Drive: How We Live Now (and Always Have) in the Future Tense* (New York: Simon & Schuster, 2004), 18.
5. Ibid., 165–66.
6. Translated and discussed by Bart D. Ehrman, *Lost Christianities* (New York: Oxford University Press, 2003), 33. (Italics added.)
7. C. S. Lewis, *The Weight of Glory*, ed. Walter Hooper (New York: Simon & Schuster, 1980), 26.
8. Brooks, *On Paradise Drive*, 199.
9. Oscar Romero, *The Violence of Love*, trans. James R. Brockman (Farmington, PA: Plough, 1998), p. 33–34.

Chapter 2: What Jesus Did Say

1. Clarence Jordan, *Sermon on the Mount* (Philadelphia: Judson Press, 1952), 17, noticed how crowds "always moved Jesus. The sight of common, ordinary folks such as one might see on any busy street, or at a football game, or in a bus station, inspired the greatest teaching ever given to humanity."
2. Joel B. Green, *The Gospel of Luke*, New International Commentary on the New Testament (Grand Rapids: Wm. B. Eerdmans Publishing Co., 1997), 265.
3. *New Testament Apocrypha*, vol. 1, ed. Wilhelm Schneemelcher, trans. R. McL. Wilson (Louisville, KY: Westminster John Knox Press, 2003), 126. (Italics added.)

4. Analyzed in comparison to Matthew 5 and Luke 6 by Dale Allison, *The Jesus Tradition in Q* (Harrisburg, PA: Trinity Press, 1997), 97. (Italics added.)

5. Ulrich Luz, *Matthew 1–7*, trans. Wilhelm C. Linss (Philadelphia: Fortress Press, 1989), 224, suggested "two concentric circles of hearers, disciples and multitudes."

6. Nicholas Lash, *Believing Three Ways in One God: A Reading of the Apostles' Creed* (Notre Dame, IN: University of Notre Dame Press, 1992), 14.

7. Jim Forest, *The Ladder of the Beatitudes* (Maryknoll, NY: Orbis Books, 1999), 2.

8. Frederick Buechner, *Whistling in the Dark* (San Francisco: HarperSanFrancisco, 1993), 19–20.

Chapter 3: Why It Matters Who Said These Words

1. William Sloane Coffin, *Credo* (Louisville, KY: Westminster John Knox Press, 2004), 156.

2. Martin Luther King Jr., *Strength to Love* (Philadelphia: Fortress Press, 1981), 53.

3. Robert Coles, *Dorothy Day: a Radical Devotion* (Reading, MA: Addison-Wesley Publishing Co., 1987), 28.

4. Ulrich Luz, *Matthew 1–7*, trans. Wilhelm C. Linss (Philadelphia: Fortress Press, 1989), 215.

5. In my *The Life We Claim: The Apostles' Creed in Preaching, Teaching and Worship* (Nashville: Abingdon Press, 2005), 85, I suggested that "I find it compelling to consider that the disciples, not an imaginative, creative bunch, with everything to lose, did what no other people who had been swayed into following a would-be Messiah (and there were plenty of them) around the countryside had done: Instead of hanging their heads and trudging home, or looking behind the next rock for a better Messiah, they plunged headlong out of the city, away from family and home, breathlessly, giddily telling the preposterous story that Jesus was indeed alive and glorified, risking (and losing) life and limb, intrepid voyagers traveling where they were incapable of going, but getting there, getting to us." See also N. T. Wright, *The Resurrection of the Son of God* (Minneapolis: Fortress Press, 2003), 557ff.

6. As narrated by Taylor Branch, in *Parting the Waters: America in the King Years, 1954–63* (New York: Simon & Schuster, 1988), 99.

7. Robert Louis Wilken, *The Spirit of Early Christian Thought: Seeking the Face of God* (New Haven, CT: Yale University Press, 2003), 278.

Chapter 4: Blessed

1. Robert Louis Wilken, *The Spirit of Early Christian Thought: Seeking the Face of God* (New Haven, CT: Yale University Press, 2003), 273.

2. Frederick Dale Bruner, *Matthew*, vol. 1, *The Christbook, Matthew 1–12* (Dallas: Word Books, 1987), 152.

3. Tom Wright, *Matthew for Everyone, Part 1* (Louisville, KY: Westminster John Knox Press, 2002), 36.

4. Bruce H. Wilkinson, *The Prayer of Jabez: Breaking Through to the Blessed Life* (Sisters: Multnomah, OR: 2000), 25–27.

5. J. R. R. Tolkien, *The Fellowship of the Ring* (New York: Ballantine Books, 1965), 212.

Chapter 5: Poor in Spirit

1. Richard Bauckham, for instance, argues compellingly that Joanna, the wife of Herod's powerful and wealthy steward Chuza, heard Jesus on this preaching tour, perhaps was healed, left her luxurious home in Tiberias, and became a disciple. See *Gospel Women: Studies of the Named Women in the Gospels* (Grand Rapids: Wm. B. Eerdmans Publishing Co., 2002), 109–202.

2. Jim Forest, *The Ladder of the Beatitudes* (Maryknoll, NY: Orbis Books, 1999), 22.

3. Frederick Buechner, *The Sacred Journey* (New York: Harper & Row, 1982), 46.

4. Clarence Jordan, *Sermon on the Mount* (Philadelphia: Judson Press, 1952), 20.

5. Gustavo Gutiérrez, *The God of Life* (Maryknoll, NY: Orbis Books, 1991), 121; see Dale C. Allison, *The Sermon on the Mount: Inspiring the Moral Imagination* (New York: Crossroad, 1999), 45.

6. Henri Nouwen, *The Return of the Prodigal Son: A Story of Homecoming* (New York: Doubleday, 1992), 79, probes this haunting question in some depth. Thomas Merton, *New Seeds of Contemplation* (New York: New Directions, 1961), 58, said, "A man who is not stripped poor and naked within his own soul will unconsciously tend to do the works he has to do for his own sake rather than for the glory of God. He will be virtuous not because he loves God's will but because he wants to admire his own virtues. But every moment of the day will bring him some frustration that will make him bitter and impatient and in his impatience he will be discovered."

7. Merton, *New Seeds of Contemplation*, 263–64.

8. Marilynne Robinson, *Gilead* (New York: Farrar, Straus & Giroux, 2004), 31.

9. W. D. Davies and Dale Allison, *A Critical and Exegetical Commentary on the Gospel According to St. Matthew*, vol. 1, International Critical Commentary (Edinburgh: T.&T. Clark, 1989), 389.

10. Leonhard Goppelt, *Theology of the New Testament*, vol. 1 (Grand Rapids: Wm. B. Eerdmans Publishing Co., 1981), 68.

11. Frederick Buechner, *The Clown in the Belfry: Writings on Faith and Fiction* (San Francisco: HarperCollins, 1992), 152.

Chapter 6: Those Who Mourn

1. Nicholas Wolterstorff, *Lament for a Son* (Grand Rapids: Wm. B. Eerdmans Publishing Co., 1987), 5.
2. Ibid., 81.
3. Ibid., 26.
4. Ibid., 85–86.
5. Richard Rohr, *Jesus' Plan for a New World: The Sermon on the Mount* (Cincinnati: St. Anthony Messenger, 1996), 133.
6. Joel B. Green, *The Gospel of Luke*, New International Commentary on the New Testament (Grand Rapids: Wm. B. Eerdmans Publishing Co., 1997), 267. Søren Kierkegaard once wrote that "to the frivolous, Christianity is certainly not glad tidings, for it wishes first of all to make them serious" (*The Journals of Søren Kierkegaard*, trans. Alexander Dru [London: Oxford University Press, 1938], 220).
7. Clarence Jordan, *Sermon on the Mount* (Philadelphia: Judson Press, 1952), 23.
8. Ibid.

Chapter 7: The Meek

1. Celsus, Christianity's most famous critic in the second century, is echoed by Nietzsche, modernity's harshest critic, who saw Christianity as a set of values that fit the weakest but are cruelly imposed on the strong, leading us to despise happiness and strength (*Genealogy of Morals* [New York: Vintage Books, 1969], 33–34). David Bentley Hart, *The Beauty of the Infinite: The Aesthetics of Christian Truth* (Grand Rapids: Wm. B. Eerdmans Publishing Co., 2003), 126, has made a fascinating reappraisal of the value of Nietzsche's critique: "Nietzsche has bequeathed Christian thought a most beautiful gift, a needed anamnesis of itself—of its strangeness. His critique . . . brings into vivid and concentrated focus the aesthetic scandal of Christianity's origins, the great offense this new faith gave the gods of antiquity . . . a God who apparels himself in common human nature, in the form of a servant; who brings good news to those who suffer and victory to those who are as nothing; who dies like a slave and outcast without resistance; who penetrates to the very depths of hell in pursuit of those he loved; who persists even after death not as a hero lifted up to Olympian glories, but in the company of peasants, breaking bread with them and offering them the solace of his wounds."
2. W. D. Davies and Dale Allison, *A Critical and Exegetical Commentary on the Gospel According to St. Matthew*, vol. 1 (Edinburgh: T.&T. Clark, 1989), 449, write that the meek "are not so much actively seeking to avoid hubris (an attitude) as they are, as a matter of fact, powerless in the eyes of the world (a condition)."

3. Thomas Merton, *New Seeds of Contemplation* (New York: New Directions, 1961), 189. Elsewhere, Merton, *Thoughts in Solitude* (New York: Noonday, 1956), 65, adds, "Humility is a virtue, not a neurosis. . . . Humility sets us free to do what is really good, by showing us our *illusions* and withdrawing our will from what was only an *apparent* good."

4. George Eliot, *Adam Bede* (New York: Signet Books, 1961), 62.

5. Jim Forest, *The Ladder of the Beatitudes* (Maryknoll, NY: Orbis Books, 1999), 50.

6. John Calvin, *Commentary on the Book of Psalms*, trans. J. Anderson (Grand Rapids: Wm. B. Eerdmans Publishing Co., 1949), xl, shares this autobiographical marvel: "From so profound an abyss of mire, God by a sudden conversion subdued and brought my mind to a teachable frame. . . . Having thus received some taste and knowledge of true godliness, I was immediately inflamed with so intense a desire to make progress." For a discussion of this "docile" attitude in relation to Christian education, see Richard Robert Osmer, *A Teachable Spirit: Recovering the Teaching Office in the Church* (Louisville, KY: Westminster/John Knox Press, 1990).

7. Ralph C. Wood, *The Gospel According to Tolkien: Visions of the Kingdom in Middle-Earth* (Louisville, KY: Westminster John Knox Press, 2003), 24.

8. J. R. R. Tolkien, *The Hobbit* (New York: Ballantine Books, 1966), 16.

9. J. R. R. Tolkien, *The Fellowship of the Ring* (New York: Ballantine Books, 1965), 21. Tolkien once told an interviewer, "The Hobbits are just rustic English people, made small in size because it reflects the generally small reach of their imagination—not the small reach of their courage or latent power" (Humphrey Carpenter, *J.R.R. Tolkien: A Biography* [Boston: Houghton Mifflin Co., 1977], 180). Tolkien himself preferred a small life with small pleasures; he was uncomfortable with fame or fortune, and spoke of "the sanctification of the humble" (*The Letters of J.R.R. Tolkien*, ed. Humphrey Carpenter [Boston: Houghton Mifflin Co., 2000], 237).

10. Tolkien, *Fellowship of the Ring*, 283.

11. Quoted, dated, and discussed in Gerhard O. Forde, *On Being a Theologian of the Cross: Reflections on Luther's Heidelberg Disputation, 1518* (Grand Rapids: Wm. B. Eerdmans Publishing Co., 1997), 62.

12. Tolkien, *Fellowship of the Ring*, 282–83.

13. Forest, *Ladder of the Beatitudes*, 55; the story comes from *The Sayings of the Desert Fathers: Alphabetical Collection*, trans. Benedicta Ward (London: Mowbray, 1984), 129–30.

14. See Forest, *Ladder of the Beatitudes*, 59; Augustine's words are taken from his third sermon on the Sermon on the Mount.

15. David Halberstam, *The Children* (New York: Fawcett Book Group, 1998), 139–40.

Chapter 8: Hunger and Thirst

1. Barry Schwartz, *The Paradox of Choice: Why More Is Less* (New York: HarperCollins, 2004), 1–2.
2. Schwartz, *The Paradox of Choice*, 109.
3. Maggie Ross, *The Fountain and the Furnace* (New York: Paulist Press, 1987), 80.
4. Mark Helprin, "First Russian Summer," in *A Dove of the East and Other Stories* (San Diego, CA: Harcourt Brace & Co., 1975), 33.
5. Pat Conroy, *The Lords of Discipline* (New York: Bantam Books, 1982), 55.
6. Jean Danielou, *From Glory to Glory: Texts from Gregory of Nyssa's Mystical Writings*, trans. Herbert Musurillo (Crestwood, NY: St. Vladimir's Press, 2001), 56. Gregory notes that "desire grows in proportion with [our] progress to each new stage of development. [We] always seem to be beginning anew" (p. 68).
7. Ibid., 45–46. Rowan Greer, *Christian Life and Christian Hope: Raids on the Inarticulate* (New York: Herder & Herder, 2001), 105, adds that "God satisfies our yearning for him and in doing so creates in us an ever greater yearning."
8. Discussed well by Kelly S. Johnson, in *The Blackwell Companion to Christian Ethics*, ed. Stanley Hauerwas and Samuel Wells (Oxford: Basil Blackwell Publisher, 2004), 235.
9. See Paul Elie, *The Life You Save May Be Your Own* (New York: Farrar, Straus & Giroux, 2003), 301.

Chapter 9: Merciful

1. Henri Nouwen, *The Return of the Prodigal Son: A Story of Homecoming* (New York: Doubleday, 1992), 12.
2. Ibid., 40.
3. Fleming Rutledge, *The Battle for Middle-Earth: Tolkien's Divine Design in The Lord of the Rings* (Grand Rapids: Wm. B. Eerdmans Publishing Co., 2004), 61ff, has written eloquently on the way Mercy and Pity (which Tolkien capitalizes to indicate not only their importance but the divine source from which they come) play out in *The Lord of the Rings*, especially when Frodo wishes Gollum were dead. Gandalf replies, "Many that live deserve death. And some that die deserve life. Can you give it to them? Then do not be too eager to deal out death in judgment. . . . I have not much hope that Gollum can be cured before he dies, but there is a chance of it. And he is bound up with the fate of the Ring. My heart tells me that he has some part to play yet, for good or ill, before the end; and when that comes, the pity of Bilbo may rule the fate of many—yours not least. In any case we did not kill him; he is very old and very wretched." Rutledge

wisely links this to Shakespeare's famous eloquence in *The Merchant of Venice*, Act IV, scene 1:

> The quality of mercy is not strained;
> It droppeth as the gentle rain from heaven
> Upon the place beneath. It is twice blest;
> It blesseth him that gives, and him that takes.
> . . . .
> Though justice be thy plea, consider this,
> That, in the course of justice, none of us
> Should see salvation. We do pray for mercy;
> And that same prayer doth teach us all to render
> The deeds of mercy.

4. Dietrich Bonhoeffer, *The Cost of Discipleship*, rev. ed., trans. R. H. Fuller (New York: Macmillan Co., 1959), 124–25.
5. Dietrich Bonhoeffer, *Life Together*, trans. John W. Doberstein (New York: Harper & Brothers, 1954), 95.
6. Wendy Farley, *Tragic Vision and Divine Compassion: A Contemporary Theodicy* (Louisville, KY: Westminster/John Knox Press, 1990), 76.

Chapter 10: Pure in Heart

1. Anna Quindlen, *One True Thing* (New York: Dell Publishing Co., 1994), 350.
2. Ibid., 382–83.
3. Marilynne Robinson, *Gilead* (New York: Farrar, Strauss & Giroux, 2004), 30.
4. Jean Leclercq, *The Love of Learning and the Desire for God*, trans. Catherine Misrahi (New York: Fordham University Press, 1982), 266.
5. Dietrich Bonhoeffer, *The Cost of Discipleship*, rev. ed., trans. R.H. Fuller (New York: Macmillan Co., 1959), 125.
6. Jim Forest, *The Ladder of the Beatitudes* (Maryknoll, NY: Orbis Books, 1999), 92.
7. Rian Malan, *My Traitor's Heart: A South African Exile Returns to Face His Country, His Tribe, and His Conscience* (New York: Vintage, 1990), 409.
8. Thomas Merton, *Contemplative Prayer* (New York: Bantam Books, 1969), 68.
9. Augustine, *The City of God*, trans. Henry Bettenson (Baltimore: Penguin Books, 1972), 1082ff.
10. Ibid., 1091.
11. *My Life for the Poor: The Story of Mother Teresa in Her Own Words*, ed. José L. González-Balado and Janet N. Playfoot (San Francisco: Harper & Row, 1985), 15.

12. Mother Teresa, *Words to Love By* (Notre Dame, IN: Ave Maria Press, 1983), 80.

Chapter 11: Peacemakers

1. Dietrich Bonhoeffer, *The Cost of Discipleship*, rev. ed., trans. R. H. Fuller (New York: Macmillan Co., 1959), 126, clarifies Jesus' point: "They must not only *have* peace, but *make* it."
2. Jim Forest, *The Ladder of the Beatitudes* (Maryknoll, NY: Orbis Books, 1999), 112.
3. Dietrich Bonhoeffer, *No Rusty Swords*, trans. John Bowden, ed. Edwin Robertson (New York: Harper & Brothers, 1956), 168, discussed probingly by Stanley Hauerwas in *Performing the Faith: Bonhoeffer and the Practice of Nonviolence* (Grand Rapids: Brazos, 2004), 13–72.
4. Forest, *Ladder of the Beatitudes*, 112.
5. Martin Luther King Jr., *Strength to Love* (Philadelphia: Fortress Press, 1981), 53.
6. Bonhoeffer, *Cost of Discipleship*, 126.
7. Bonhoeffer, *No Rusty Swords*, 168, also explored well by Hauerwas, *Performing the Faith*, 13–72.
8. Frederick Buechner, *Wishful Thinking: A Theological ABC* (New York: Harper & Row, 1973), 29.
9. John Irving, *The World According to Garp* (New York: Ballantine Books, 1976), 380–81.
10. Martin Luther King Jr., *A Testament of Hope*, ed. James Washington (New York: Harper & Row, 1986), 219.
11. Clarence Jordan, *Sermon on the Mount* (Philadelphia: Judson Press, 1952), 20.
12. Peter Storey, *With God in the Crucible: Preaching Costly Discipleship* (Nashville: Abingdon Press, 2002), 29.

Chapter 12: Persecuted

1. "Luke has not spiritualized the condition of the disciples as Matthew has done. . . . Rather, poverty, hunger, weeping, hatred, and ostracism characterize the real condition of the Christian disciples whom Jesus declares 'blessed'" (Joseph Fitzmyer, *The Gospel According to Luke I–IX* [Garden City, NY: Doubleday & Co., 1981], 631).
2. Quoted and discussed by Ramsay MacMullen, *Christianizing the Roman Empire (A.D. 100–400)* (New Haven, CT: Yale University Press, 1984), 34.
3. Michael Grant, *Gladiators* (London: Penguin Books, 1967), 101. Grant argues that the Christians, acting formally at the Council of Nicaea, eventually forced the abolition of gladiators' games.

4. Tertullian, "Apology," in *Apologetical Works*, Fathers of the Church, vol. 10, trans. Rudolph Arbesmann (New York: Fathers of the Church, Inc., 1950), 125.

5. *A New Eusebius*, ed. J. Stevenson (London: SPCK, 1957), 21.

6. G. K. Chesterton, *What's Wrong with the World* (Fort Collins, CO: Ignatius Press, 1994), 38.

7. Dietrich Bonhoeffer, *The Cost of Discipleship*, rev. ed., trans. R. H. Fuller (New York: Macmillan Co., 1959), 45–47.

8. See Heiko Oberman, *Luther: Man Between God and the Devil*, trans. Eileen Walliser-Schwarzbart (New York: Image Books, 1992), 106.

9. Quoted by James Cone in *Martyrdom Today*, ed. Johannes Baptist-Metz and Edward Schillebeeckx (New York: Seabury Press, 1983), 76.

10. Christopher Lasch, *The True and Only Heaven: Progress and Its Critics* (New York: W.W. Norton & Co., 1991), 80–81.

11. Reinhold Niebuhr, *The Irony of American History* (New York: Charles Scribner's Sons, 1952), 63.

12. *The Hidden Ground of Love: Letters by Thomas Merton*, ed. William Shannon (San Diego, CA: Harcourt Brace Jovanovich, 1993), 294.

13. Mother Teresa, *A Simple Path*, compiled by Lucinda Vardey (New York: Ballantine Books, 1995), 185.

Chapter 13: Saints and Heroes

1. Nicholas Lash, "Performing the Scriptures," *Theology on the Way to Emmaus* (London: SCM Press, 1986), 42.

2. David Bentley Hart, *The Beauty of the Infinite*, 441, asserts that our persuasion "must always assume the shape of the gift he is."

3. Murray Bodo, *The Way of St. Francis* (New York: Image, 1984), 21.

4. G. K. Chesterton, *St. Francis of Assisi* (Garden City, NY: Image Books, 1957), 40, 47.

5. Carlo Carretto, *I, Francis*, trans. Robert R. Barr (Maryknoll, NY: Orbis Books, 1985), 75.

6. Murray Bodo, *Juniper: Friend of Francis, Fool of God* (Cincinnati: St. Anthony Messenger Press, 1983), 28.

7. To learn more about Thérèse, see my *Servants, Misfits and Martyrs: Saints and Their Stories* (Nashville: Upper Room, 1999), 57–60, and footnote citations there to Guy Gaucher, *The Story of a Life: St. Thérèse of Lisieux* (San Francisco: HarperSanFrancisco, 1987).

8. Paul Elie, *The Life You Save May Be Your Own* (New York: Farrar, Straus & Giroux, 2003), ix, suggested that she "doesn't look like someone who might make you want to change your life. . . . In her castoff overcoat and kerchief Dorothy Day might be a nun or a social worker, not a radical under surveillance by the FBI." For more of what follows on Day, with references, see my *Servants, Misfits and Martyrs*, 43–48.

9. Jim Forest, *Love Is the Measure: A Biography of Dorothy Day*, rev. ed. (Maryknoll, NY: Orbis Books, 1994), 135.
10. Dorothy Day, *The Long Loneliness* (1952; repr., HarperSanFrancisco, 1997), 243.
11. Forest, *Love Is the Measure*, 67.
12. Tracy Kidder, *Mountains beyond Mountains* (New York: Random House, 2003), 210.
13. Elias Chacour, *Blood Brothers* (Old Tappan, NJ: Fleming H. Revell Co., 1987).
14. James Brockman, *Romero: A Life* (Maryknoll, NY: Orbis Books, 1989), 234, 248.
15. Stanley Hauerwas, *In Good Company: The Church as Polis* (Notre Dame, IN: University of Notre Dame Press, 1995), 45–46.
16. Dietrich Bonhoeffer, *Letters and Papers from Prison*, ed. Eberhard Bethge (New York: Macmillan Co., 1971), 234.

Chapter 14: Presence of the Future

1. For more, see Ruby Payne, *A Framework for Understanding Poverty* (Highlands, TX: Aha! Process Inc., 2001).
2. Frederick Buechner, *Wishful Thinking: A Theological ABC* (New York: Harper & Row, 1973), 49f.
3. Reynolds Price, *A Whole New Life* (New York: Simon & Schuster, 2000), 57.
4. Augustine, *The City of God*, trans. Henry Bettenson (Baltimore: Penguin Books, 1972), 1082.
5. Thérèse of Lisieux, "To Live of Love," in Guy Gaucher, *The Story of a Life: St. Thérèse of Lisieux* (San Francisco: HarperSanFrancisco, 1987), 146.
6. Christopher Lasch, *The Revolt of the Elites and the Betrayal of Democracy* (New York: W.W. Norton & Co., 1995), 159.
7. Martin Luther King Jr., *A Testament of Hope*, ed. James Washington (New York: Harper & Row, 1986), 282, on the night before he was killed, preached, "It's alright to talk about 'long white robes over yonder,' in all of its symbolism. But ultimately people want some suits and dresses and shoes to wear down here. It's alright to talk about 'streets flowing with milk and honey,' but God has commanded us to be concerned about the slums down here, and his children who can't eat three square meals a day. It's alright to talk about the new Jerusalem, but one day, God's preacher must talk about the New York, the new Atlanta, the new Philadelphia, the new Los Angeles, the new Memphis, Tennessee."
8. Marilynne Robinson, *Gilead* (New York: Farrar, Straus & Giroux, 2004), 57.
9. Fleming Rutledge, *The Battle for Middle-Earth: Tolkien's Divine Design in The Lord of the Rings* (Grand Rapids: Wm. B. Eerdmans

Co., 2004), 94, n. 7, analyzing Tolkien's *Lord of the Rings* trilogy, speaks of "transvision . . . because it suggests looking *through* or *beyond* present reality (the surface narrative, if you will) to the greater, eternal reality (the deep narrative), so that one sees both at the same time. . . . We see *through* the sufferings of the present *into* the future that God has already prepared for us."

10. Evelyn Underhill, *The Ways of the Spirit* (New York: Crossroad, 1996), 73.

11. C. S. Lewis, *Surprised by Joy: The Shape of My Early Life* (New York: Harcourt, 1955), 17–18.

Further Reading

Allison, Dale C. *The Sermon on the Mount: Inspiring the Moral Imagination.* New York: Crossroad, 1999.

Bonhoeffer, Dietrich. *The Cost of Discipleship.* Rev. ed. Translated by R. H. Fuller. New York: Macmillan Co., 1959.

Forest, Jim. *The Ladder of the Beatitudes.* Maryknoll, NY: Orbis Books, 1999.

Jordan, Clarence. *Sermon on the Mount.* Philadelphia: Judson Press, 1952.

Luz, Ulrich. *Matthew 1–7.* Translated by Wilhelm C. Linss. Minneapolis: Augsburg, 1989.